THE DEED OF LIFE

"Man is born to live, not to prepare for life. Life itself, the phenomenon of life, the gift of life, is so breath-takingly serious!"

DOCTOR ZHIVAGO

THE DEED OF LIFE

THE NOVELS AND TALES OF

D. H. LAWRENCE

By JULIAN MOYNAHAN

PRINCETON, NEW JERSEY
PRINCETON UNIVERSITY PRESS

Copyright © 1963 by Princeton University Press

ALL RIGHTS RESERVED

L. C. Card: 63-9986

ISBN 0-691-01257-1 (paperback edn.)

ISBN 0-691-06023-1 (hardcover edn.)

First PRINCETON PAPERBACK Edition, 1966

Second Printing, 1972

Printed in the United States of America
by Princeton University Press, Princeton, N.J.

IN MEMORY OF

John F. McAndrew

ACKNOWLEDGEMENTS

I AM INDEBTED to the administration and the English Department of Princeton University for several research grants and the award of a Bicentennial Preceptorship which provided me with free time to finish this book. I am also grateful for the material aid provided by a grant from the American Council of Learned Societies.

Portions of Parts IV and V have already appeared in somewhat different form as essays in *English Literary History* and *Modern Fiction Studies*.

I am grateful to Harry T. Levin and Reuben A. Brower of Harvard who supervised my doctoral dissertation on Lawrence and have influenced my attitude toward his fiction and toward the writing of criticism very substantially. The plan of this book precludes much reference to the numerous critical and biographical studies of Lawrence already in print from which I have profited. Here I wish to acknowledge a particular debt to the biographical researches and writings of Harry T. Moore and Edward Nehls and to the criticism of F. R. Leavis, Graham Hough, Mark Schorer, Mark Spilka, Dorothy Van Ghent, A. Alvarez, Eliseo Vivas, and Richard Rees.

And I wish to thank my wife Elizabeth Moynahan for her willingness to give D. H. Lawrence house room over the past nine or ten years.

CONTENTS

CONTENTS

THE DEED OF LIFE

INTRODUCTION

THIS BOOK is a study of Lawrence's major works of fiction[1] as works of art. While I believe that all valuable fiction illuminates the muddle of the human condition and is animated by deep insight into human behavior and into the workings of society, I have tried to avoid a preoccupation with two intertwined concerns that have dominated most previous discussion of this important modern writer: the concern with Lawrence's prophetic message; the polemical effort to defend or attack the moral significance of Lawrence's message and career. There are a few people still alive in Taos, New Mexico, who believe Lawrence will return from the dead within the forseeable future to survey our world from a judgment seat presumably located in the sanctuary of the Phoenix Shrine on Mt. Lobos. There are people in Taos and elsewhere who believe he is in hell and will continue to reside there forever. A great poet and critic, Mr. T. S. Eliot, believes that Lawrence was incapable of what is ordinarily meant by thinking. Another great critic, Mr. F. R. Leavis, believes that his thought was incomparably the richest and most sustained effort to comprehend the varied ills and promises of modern life by any twentieth century writer. All these opinions are not closely relevant to my interest in Lawrence. I care mainly about the creative

[1] Throughout this book page numbers following all extended quotations from Lawrence's fiction normally refer to volumes of *The Phoenix Edition of D. H. Lawrence* (London: Heinemann, 1954-). Since Heinemann's has not yet replaced its expurgated edition of *Lady Chatterley's Lover* with the unexpurgated text, my page references for that novel refer to "The Author's Unabridged Popular Edition" (Paris, 1929). I omit page references altogether when quoting from the two volumes of Lawrence's short novels because the pagination of these volumes is discontinuous and therefore misleading.

results of Lawrence's sustained creative practice over two decades in the art of fiction.

Naturally, this study brings certain other assumptions into play which should be indicated at the beginning not only to disarm or arm the critics of criticism, but also to designate for less professionally involved readers the area of the writer's prejudices and commitments.

D. H. Lawrence's novels and shorter tales are incomparably his most important and interesting work. He was a good poet, especially in the nonrhyming, cadenced verse of *Birds, Beasts and Flowers* and *Last Poems*. He was extraordinarily gifted as a writer of descriptive and expository essays. His four travel books represent a remarkable body of work in a semi-fictional genre which he almost might be said to have invented and which deserves the sort of systematic investigation it will inevitably receive from literary historians and theorists of the future. He spent much time in the composition of polemical-mystical essays and treatises like *Fantasia of the Unconscious*, "The Crown," and *Apocalypse* which are sometimes contemptible as coherently argued statements of thought and often interesting for particular striking insights.

Nevertheless, he was a novelist and a writer of tales first and last. Much of his other work, including the poetry, is occasional in both good and bad senses of the word. All his claims to greatness rest upon his work in the novel, novella, and short story. The evidence is compelling that throughout his career he saw himself as, understood his profession as that of a novelist. Furthermore, the merest glance at his own published comments on the novel as a literary form reveal he regarded it unconditionally as the highest art form, the "one bright book of life," the one form of virtually unlimited expressive potentiality. Lawrence must stand or fall as a novelist, not as a poet, essayist,

letter writer, mystagogue, or professional traveler. No doubt
he would have wanted it that way.

D. H. Lawrence is a great novelist. We are dealing with
a form protean in the extreme, to which nearly every liberty
has been permitted, that has developed as a genre by a
process of continuous, quasi-Trotskyist revolution or self-
transformation; and therefore it would be foolish to give
a precise recipe for the great novel or novelist. I put forward
Lawrence's claim to greatness on two grounds. His best
work is continuous with the richest traditions of English
fiction beginning with Richardson if not with Defoe. By
tradition here is meant a set of techniques, thematic pre-
occupations, styles in language, styles in the creation of
mood and atmosphere, story archetypes, character archetypes, normative conventions of narrative and scene organization, etc. etc., which are blended and reblended by all
practitioners of serious fiction in English. In short, I am
speaking of a literary tradition, a tradition of literary practitioners, not of a moral tradition of the English novel
construed as a kind of club admitting five or six true-blue
candidates while blackballing the rest on grounds of idle
and disorderly, or lewd and lascivious behavior.

Secondly, Lawrence's best work modifies tradition by
adding something new. When a great novelist has completed his life work he leaves the possibilities of the form
drastically altered. He has redefined certain conventions,
broken others, and invented some new ones as well. The
form, conceived of as an expressive instrument (in the
sense that a human body is an instrument for work, suffering, and delight), has altered its dimensions, developed
new powers, grown out in one direction, shrunken or become dessicated in another. In the context of tradition the
great novelist is both a phenomenon of continuity and
growth and a phenomenon of discontinuity and unlooked

for change; or, as Lawrence put it so well in another connection, the task of the artist is "to discover or invent a new
world within the known world," the "known world" standing here for the developed form at any given moment of its
history, the "new world" standing for what has been in-
novated by any given major novelist.

Lawrence was an uneven novelist. Some of his works of
fiction are not on a level with his best works of fiction. Some
of his best novels and stories contain lapses of technique,
insight, and taste. Some of the fiction that he regarded as
major is undeniably bad. In the last category *The Plumed
Serpent* should be cited before anything else. Since aesthetic
practice in the novel has been notoriously uneven throughout its history these facts need no apology. *Pamela* is a
blend of refined psychological drama, subtle social comedy,
lubricious and crude melodrama, and outrageous bourgeois
moralizing. Dickens' neurotic pathos, his vapid celebrations
of cheery little domestic interiors are in conflict with his
deep insight into the recesses of the human spirit from
which proliferating impulses of violence, lust, envy, and
hatred make their way disguised into human affairs to cast
a blighting shadow. The odd streak of dry cruelty in Jane
Austen had come to color so much of her outlook by the
time she wrote *Persuasion* that it nearly spoiled the last of
the most nearly perfect set of novels composed by any
English writer.

The condition is normal. In the best novelists there is
often much to complain of: whether it is Dostoevsky's
febrile humor and technical slovenliness (*The Possessed*
begins in the first person and ends essentially in the third),
Flaubert's superabundance of *mots justes*, Tolstoi's religious
morbidity, the compulsive pedantry of Joyce's *Ulysses*,
weighing down his witty and humane story of Dublin men
and women, or the *longueurs* of Proust's protracted obses-

sion with Marcel's protracted obsession with Albertine. Yet
the career of every one of these writers marked an epoch in
the history of the novel and in the history of European
man's struggle to understand himself and society.

The main consequence of the fact of Lawrence's uneven-
ness for this book has been my distribution of emphasis.
*Sons and Lovers, The Rainbow, Women in Love, The Lost
Girl*, and *Lady Chatterley's Lover* stand out superior in
interest and achievement and are given the more extended
treatment. The so-called leadership group of novels—
Aaron's Rod, Kangaroo, and *The Plumed Serpent*—written in the early to middle 1920's, are treated together in
a single chapter. The assumption is that they are unsuccessful books, and the task of this chapter is less to demonstrate
copiously their obvious shortcomings than to account diag-
nostically for the failure. The section devoted to the shorter
tales also emphasizes the best work, duplicating on a smaller
scale the plan of the rest of the book. This study, then, is a
compromise between a purely intensive approach and a
broad survey of a total body of work. This compromise is
necessary in order to bring forward Lawrence's most significant writing and also show to some extent the variety,
connectedness, and massiveness of his work as a whole.

My method of criticism intends to be unsystematic and as
flexible as possible. Early criticism, the books and essays
written approximately between 1925 and 1950, was often
produced by people whose concern was more with Lawrence
as a salvationist, prophet, and personality than with Lawrence as a literary man. More recently the trend has been
toward studies based on rather narrowly defined critical
methodologies and standards: studies of symbolism in the
novels; Lawrence from the standpoint of Jungian archetypes, Lawrence from the moralizing viewpoint of the
Cambridge School of English; and no doubt we shall soon

have a book on Lawrence from the political viewpoint of the English New Left. While no critic can discuss Lawrence's fiction without moralizing, without taking political stances, without frequent reference to symbolism, none of these approaches is exclusively suited to accomplish the perennial tasks of criticism, which are: to discriminate the formal organization of works of art; to determine the coherence and completeness of these organizations; to judge the moral, intellectual, and affective value of what has been discriminated. And of course every critic performs these tasks not *sub specie eternitatis* but fully aware of the limitations imposed on his understanding by his own weaknesses as well as by the condition of health or unhealth of the society to which he belongs.

This book will be concerned only occasionally with the question of Lawrence's extraordinary personality and with his habit of restating his creative insights as doctrinal formulae not because I subscribe to two recently discarded articles of critical faith called "the biographical fallacy," and the "intentional fallacy," but because I agree with Proust's view that the self an artist exhibits in his imaginative work is incommensurate with and transcends his everyday personality and is the only self that finally matters to the reader; because I heartily agree with Lawrence's notion that an artist does his most significant thinking in and through the imaginative designs of his art, and that therefore one must "trust the tale, not the artist." In other words, I take Lawrence to have been a professional novelist but no more than an amateur prophet and mortal man.

Nevertheless, Lawrence's novels do contain a nexus of ideas which are sometimes misunderstood and which therefore need to be defined briefly before we begin to look at the novels themselves. In *Speculations*, published in 1924 but composed before his death in the first world war, the

young English philosopher T. E. Hulme provided a con-
venient set of diagrams for this purpose. Hulme's lucid attack on humanism and romanticism as attitudes underlying
one kind of modern art has often been used against Lawrence and might readily have been used against other post-
Christian writers of the early twentieth century—for example, against Joyce, Shaw, Forster, and Yeats. I merely want
to use it to place Lawrence's work with respect to one or
two central doctrines.

According to Hulme, pre-Renaissance thought correctly
divided reality into three absolutely disjunct spheres: (1)
inanimate matter, dealt with by physical science; (2) the
organic world, dealt with by biology, psychology, and history; (3) the sphere of ethical and religious values, dealt
with by theology and the direct intuitions of faith. The
first and third spheres have an absolute character, and
knowledge about them is an absolute knowledge. The "in-
termediate zone of life" is somehow different. It is a mud-
dy zone between two absolutes, and knowledge of it remains loose and relative.

With the rise of Humanism at the Renaissance the notion of reality, and of knowledge-about-reality, as a con-
tinuum became ascendant over the idea of three disjunct
spheres. Under the stimulus of Rousseau, and of romanticism generally, the organic sphere encroached upon the
ethical and religious sphere, while an increasingly mechanistic science was manipulated to supply mechanical models
of organic phenomena. At the end of the nineteenth century there is a move away from the mechanical view of life
under the influence of Nietzsche and Bergson, but there
is no corresponding movement to reinstate the absolute distinction between the biological sphere and the ethical and
religious sphere. By 1900 the former threefold division has
contracted into a simple dualism between dead matter and

vital processes, with all values, including the strictly religious ones, subsumed under the category of the organic.
Hulme's account oversimplifies intellectual history but does
not really falsify it. His comment on where the nineteenth
century comes out is: "This is ridiculous. Biology is not
theology, nor can God be defined in terms of life."[2]

At about the same time as Hulme was saying that, Lawrence was writing *Sons and Lovers*. Of God Paul Morel
says, "I don't believe God knows such a lot about Himself.
God doesn't *know* things. He *is* things. And I'm sure He's
not soulful." A few pages later Lawrence says of Paul
Morel:

> He had shovelled away all the beliefs that would hamper
> him, had cleared the ground, and come more or less to the
> bedrock of belief that one should feel inside oneself for
> right and wrong, and should have the patience to gradually
> realise one's God. Now life interested him more.   (p. 256)

The issue could not be drawn more clearly. For Hulme,
life is a welter upon which value must be imposed from
above and beyond. The obvious model is Moses on Mount
Sinai accepting the rigid tables of the law from a hidden
Creator while the Israelites tumble about the golden calf
on the sands below. For Lawrence, values are discovered
or created outright in the act of living. At the risk of
momentarily distorting religious legend let us pretend that
the calf was not a brazen image but alive and bawling, that
the Israelites were treading a solemn measure celebrating
the God that *is* things because life interested them more
than stone tablets from an inscrutable source.

Lawrence never abandoned the conviction that life creates
value and is somehow self-sanctioning. His novels were

[2] T. E. Hulme, *Speculations: Essays on Humanism and the Philosophy
of Art*, ed. Herbert Read, 2d ed. (London: Routledge and Kegan Paul,
1936), p. 8.

experiments testing that hypothesis in a variety of contexts: "inside oneself," in personal relations, in the larger contexts of society, economics, and politics, in the context which is at once the largest of all and yet the least abstracted from the single self, that of organic processes. His conclusions are not always firm or clear, and he began the enterprise rather more encumbered with personal disadvantages than anyone but an enemy might wish. Yet he seems to have faced all the really difficult problems raised by his doctrinal position; for instance, the problem of how to reconcile the lively values of growth, health, and wholesomeness with the indisputable facts of human destructiveness in personal relations, in society at large, and, since the recent advent of nuclear weapons technology it can be added, against nature. As a novelist, and as a moralist as well, he conducted his search in the terms of common life. He looked more closely than any other modern writer in English at the knotty fibers of human feeling and instinct which tie ordinary men to one another, out of which the strange texture of human experience is woven, for life or for death. That is his paramount importance.

PART I

THE SEARCH FOR FORM

THE WHITE PEACOCK
THE TRESPASSER
SONS AND LOVERS

1

THE WHITE PEACOCK was begun in 1906 when Lawrence was a university student of twenty and completed in
1909 when he was teaching school at Croyden. *The Trespasser*, begun in the spring of 1910, was rewritten and completed in February 1912, after an interruption because of
a serious illness following close upon the death of Lawrence's mother. *Sons and Lovers*, in its earliest version
called *Paul Morel*, had been under way as early as October 1910 and had been finished through a first draft within
the next twelve months. In May 1912 Lawrence eloped
to Germany with Frieda Weekley and produced the final
draft of *Sons and Lovers* by November of the same year,
while living with her at Gargnano, in the lake country of
northern Italy. With the publication of that book Lawrence altered the course of the English novel. *Sons and
Lovers*, whatever its defects, is instantly recognizable as a
major renewal of narrative form, as such strictly comparable
to the first significant work by any leading English novelist
of the past two and a quarter centuries.

There is always something shocking about the emergence
of an artistic genius. In Lawrence's case, there is something
almost scandalous. In what sense scandalous? When he
began to write in 1906 he was a hapless provincial from
a colliery village. His health was delicate and he was under the thumb of a strong-minded mother. As late as 1911
his position and prospects had deteriorated, if anything. He
had proved himself a competent master of secondary school
students, but his health had broken under the strain of his
mother's sufferings in cancer; also, he was mired in a mu-
tually obfuscating relation with his childhood sweetheart
Jessie Chambers, who had so much influence over him

that he accepted her as a virtual collaborator while writing *Paul Morel*. What is more to the point, his first novel had been third-rate and his second would be worse. Fascinating as they become *after* his emergence as a great writer, neither book offers the remotest hint that such a break-through would ever be possible. Nowadays it might be hard to find a publisher for them, and today's editorial standards are not notably high.

And yet, only a year later Lawrence had recovered from his mother-inspired illness and had broken decisively with Jessie Chambers, the tragic prototype of the tragic Miriam in his third novel. He had put school teaching, and with it a kind of financial security, behind him for good. More important, he had found and drawn from her domestic setting in Nottingham the woman with whom he was to live out the remainder of his life. Scarcely recovered from a near-fatal illness, and with a courageous sureness that is literally astonishing, he convinced a pretty, lively, unhappily married woman, who was certainly as devoted to her children as most mothers are, that she must, for the sake of truth to feeling and the higher morality of love, abandon her children, humiliate her husband, scandalize her aristocratic German relatives—in short risk everything—for an unknown writer of two febrile novels, a few first-rate short stories, and some interesting if often rough-hewn verses. Lawrence offered Frieda nothing except his intensely moral conviction that they were to love and cleave to each other. He had no money and no social or professional status. Frieda's English life had been conducted outside the sphere of fashionable London cultural circles where open adultery might be viewed as an acceptable or even laudable way of going on. And Lawrence, regardless of his sponsorship by Ford Maddox Ford, his occasional appearances at literary dinner parties in Hampstead or

Bloomsbury, was equally unsophisticated. The resources of personal integrity on both sides from which the decision to risk everything came remain strictly unexaminable. The correctness of their joint decision emerged, like *Sons and Lovers* itself, only in the aftermath.

In Germany, Frieda went home to Metz to cope with her uneasy parents, while Lawrence hung about in lodgings, suffering but sure. Then, still waiting for her, he visited Trier and Waldbröhl. They were reunited in Munich and began their wanderings southward through the Tyrol and into northern Italy. The poem-sequence *Look! We Have Come Through!* records the pangs and compensations of that prolonged, illicit honeymoon during which both fought for and won a marriage. The drag on Frieda was mother-love. She would lie on the floor blind with grief over the loss of her children. The drag on Lawrence was mother-love. According to Harry Moore's sensitive and comprehensive account of Lawrence's work on the final draft of *Sons and Lovers*, "Frieda remembers that when Lawrence wrote of his mother's death, it made him ill, and his grief upset her, too. He told her that if his mother had lived she would not have let him love Frieda: 'But I think he got over it.' "[1]

Did he get over it? Frieda was not always so sure, even at Gargnano in the first flush of their journey through, where she wrote Lawrence an enraged note telling him to go back to his mother's apron strings and an acrid skit entitled "Paul Morel, or His Mother's Darling." The common denominator of Lawrence's first three novels is a preternatural sensitivity to the currents of feeling running between men and women. That sensitivity surely derived from Lawrence's neurotically intense awareness of the emo-

[1] *The Intelligent Heart: The Story of D. H. Lawrence*, rev. ed. (Harmondsworth, Middlesex: Penguin Books, 1960), p. 176.

tional climate of his own household, where his mother fought perpetually with his father and committed the well-nigh unforgivable sin of taking her children aside and supplying intimate, self-justifying details of her marital difficulties. Operating on a man of mere talent this fearful stimulus might have produced a homosexual stage designer or minor poet. On Lawrence the same stimulus produced: (1) the two early novels, where the burden of familial misery is fumbled with but never carried; (2) *Sons and Lovers*, where the same handicap is bravely explored and the insight it bred is released to become the driving power in subsequent books of a new, major exploration of human relationships.

At forty-five Lawrence died, burned out from tuberculosis. In *Fantasia of the Unconscious* (1922) he had written that when a male child is aroused to a passionate mother-love he is liable to contract tuberculosis of the lungs at some time in his life.[2] So it may be true that Lawrence never escaped the decisive influence of his parents' disharmony. Certainly psychoanalysis, which Lawrence's entire body of writing parallels, quarrels with, and occasionally corrects, has taught that one's earliest past can never be lived down. But psychoanalysis, which in its classical form is a philosophy of courage, also teaches that the burden of the past may sometimes be transformed into a burden of insight and achievement. The most interesting examples of these transformations are to be found in the careers of great artists. Artists are not necessarily braver than ordinary people, although the best of them always are. But they are luckier, inasmuch as the practice of their art provides them with special opportunities to turn their sufferings and shortcomings into illumination and form.

Lawrence was a brave man. He made a good marriage

[2] (New York: Thomas Seltzer, 1922), pp. 70-71.

against stacked odds and kept it going to the end. He was an artist who emerged from what he called the "death-experience" of a poor, provincial, unwholesome household to write novels full of a sense of life and health. His third novel was the first of these. Finally, he had genius, which meant he could take an incredible, scandalous leap into the dark and land in the light. The fable of the ugly duckling who turned overnight into a fierce and splendid swan is a transparent allegory of the miracle of biological growth. It can serve just as well to represent the emergence of creative genius in its first stage.

2

Lawrence's first two books are improvisations. Although their story materials were supplied by recollection as much as by invention, they took the form that Lawrence's deepest tormented feeling about the misery of the male-female relation dictated. The feeling was extraordinarily unbalanced and was not squarely faced by the young writer, with disastrous results for the coherence and truth-value of the stories. As Lawrence was to preach and practice a little while later, art demands courage and utter sincerity. The measure of the unsuccess of *The White Peacock* and *The Trespasser* is precisely the measure of the writer's emotional insecurity at the beginning of his career.

The White Peacock, employing country settings and figures based on people taken directly from the pastoral northern slope of Lawrence's half-industrialized, half-agricultural home valley outside Nottingham, depicts in a series of loosely repetitive episodes the spiritual ruin or actual physical destruction of several male characters. All are

destroyed through their inability to find a satisfactory relation with the women they court, love, and marry. As time
passes and the men sicken and decay, their women wax "ar-
rogant" . . . "imperious" . . . "strong". . . "stately." Moth-
erhood, which confers "a touch of ironical brutality" on one
important female character, is the role through which the
woman attains to full power as destroyer of men:

> The mother's dark eyes, and the baby's large, hazel eyes
> looked at me serenely. The two were very calm, very
> complete and triumphant together. In their completeness
> was a security which made me feel alone and ineffectual.
> A woman who has her child in her arms is a tower of
> strength, a beautiful, unassailable tower of strength that
> may in its turn stand quietly dealing death.   (p.289)

The nature of this deadly power is never satisfactorily
explained by the evasive, first-person narrator, Cyril Beardsall; nor does he ever attempt to account for the extraordinary weakness of the men, which causes them to go under
so readily in the sex war Lawrence envisions as the norm
of erotic and marital relations. All of the defeated males
are woefully passive and are pathologically oversensitive to
feminine rebuke and resistance. The two most important,
the farmer George Saxton and the gamekeeper Frank Annable, are also narcissistic, a trait they share with Siegmund,
the suicidal hero of *The Trespasser*. Siegmund is directly
destroyed by the active hatred of his wife and children,
but he has already lost his chance for survival during his
love idyll with Helena on the Isle of Wight, where he is
forced to recognize his failure as a lover:

> Is that why I have failed? I ought to have had her in love
> sufficiently to keep her these few days. I am not quick. I
> do not follow her or understand her swiftly enough. And
> I am always timid of compulsion. I cannot compel anybody
> to follow me. (p. 103)

6

Here suggestions of overresponsiveness and passivity combine to eliminate all hope for the broody violinist. In neither book is it ever suggested that the air might clear if the male ceased for a time to react to the slightest fluctuations of the woman's moods with terror and anxious concern; and it is never suggested that a man set up his life on the hard-headed assumption that his relations with the opposite sex are bound to be full of tribulations and misunderstandings.

Women undermine men's hold on life. This is a *donné* of both novels which is only occasionally stated direct but constantly and compulsively enacted. In *The White Peacock* George Saxton is made physically ill by Letty's refusal of his marriage proposal and becomes a chronic alcoholic after entering into a loveless marriage with his cousin. But the crucial case is that of the gamekeeper. Viewed superficially, Annable appears the one man in the novel who has triumphed in the sex war. As the father of a wild brood of children whom he designates by animal labels, ferrets, weasels, young foxes; and as the brutally dominant husband of a drab, submissive, and demoralized woman, he would seem to have saved his manhood by developing a callous and masterful attitude. Yet it emerges quickly enough as we follow his fiercely anti-feminine invective and discover his early history of marital misfortune with Lady Chrystabel that he suffers under the same blight as the other males. When the Lady discarded him after years of dominating him, he put on servant's clothes and took to the woods. While appearing to flourish there like some wild thing, he has actually lost his will to live. His death in the quarry rockfall merely acts out an admission he had made to Cyril the day before: "I feel somehow, as if I were at an end."

Taken together, these novels, with their gothic effects

7

and *fin-de-siècle* lusciousness of tone and imagery, are adolescent fantasies adumbrating the domestic "death-experience" of the Lawrence household. But *The White Peacock*, taken by itself, is a little more than that. It is in effect a stagnant pool dimly reflecting some of Lawrence's later emphases. The problem is how to show this without exaggerating the novel's claims on our attention.

The story is held together by the narrator's decade-long search for a life-sustaining relation to others which he never finds, and the several episodes of sexual conflict are framed by that search. As a character Cyril cannot be taken very seriously and at best seems only half-created. For part of the time he is merely being used to work off Lawrence's feelings of youthful *weltschmertz*. But his malaise goes deeper. Cyril's starting point is at the bedside of his father, who has just died of alcoholism after years of morose, beggarly wandering. Here the son experiences a self-annihilating feeling of isolation and lostness: "I felt the great wild pity, and a sense of terror, and a sense of horror, and a sense of awful littleness and loneliness among a great empty space. I felt beyond myself as if I were a mere fleck drifting unconsciously through the dark" (pp. 36-37). This intuition, which anticipates Paul Morel's vision of nullity at the end of *Sons and Lovers*, recurs frequently to him and is clearly the threat forcing this extraordinarily detached figure to renew sporadically his efforts to integrate himself with life. It also explains the extreme diffidence with which he conducts the search; for both isolation and a bad sort of connection come to the same thing—decay and death.

During his search Cyril turns to a woman, Emily Saxton, but their friendship comes to nothing, partly because they are too shy and inhibited with each other, partly because Lawrence has so little interest in the love affair that he drops it out of the novel about a third of the way through. With greater energy Cyril turns to two men, George Saxton and the gamekeeper, Frank Annable. These associations are offered us as being more "natural" than the association with woman. Cyril is attracted to George by "the movement of active life" he demonstrates in his physical labor on the farm and wishes to connect himself with that movement. He is drawn to Annable by the man's immense physical vigor and animalism. Annable treats Cyril in a fatherly fashion. In their association Cyril apparently finds an image of masculine vigor to replace the ravaged father, Frank Beardsall.

Yet these relations represent no wholesome solution to Cyril's problem. For one thing, neither George nor the gamekeeper are the integrated natural men they appear to be. As soon as George marries and moves off the land he begins to decay. Annable, despite his break with organized society where the mothers deal death, has already been sickened unto death by women. And there is a strong flavor of homoeroticism in the narrator's "almost passionate" attachment to George Saxton and in his admiration of the gamekeeper's physique. Lawrence is at once more explicit and less optimistic about innocent homosexuality in a natural setting than the classic American authors Mr. Leslie Fiedler analyzed recently in *Love and Death in the American Novel*.[3] In the bathing scene of the chapter called "A Poem of Friendship," George embraces Cyril's naked body and rubs him "briskly, as if I were a child, or rather, a woman he loved and did not fear. . . . When he had rubbed me all warm, he let me go, and we looked at each other with eyes of still laughter, and our love was perfect for a moment, more perfect than any love I have known since,

[3] (New York: Criterion Books, 1960).

either for man or woman" (p. 222). But even though this is the only unqualifiedly tender scene in the entire book, neither the characters involved nor the author are willing to build an enduring relation upon it.

When the human connection fails him, Cyril turns to nature to gain some solace through his self-identification with its vital rhythms. But he cannot find a saving connection for himself in nature precisely because he is so withdrawn from other human beings. After all, he cannot mate with the flowers, trees, swans, plough horses, and little animals he spends so much time describing. Thus, when he sees and exquisitely describes two baby larks lying serenely at ease in a nest laid in the print left on wet ground by a horse's hoof, he can only conclude by expressing envy of their security and lamenting his aloneness. At the end of the book he merges with the Renfrew family group as they close ranks against the despised alcoholic brother-in-law, George Saxton. But this solidarity with the Renfrews is spurious. He is far closer to George than he admits, if we translate his evasiveness as a narrator and as a character into terms of alienation from the milieu in which women rule, "quiet and self-assured," while their menfolk either deteriorate in servitude or die outright. In a novel which assumes there is no life without relatedness of a wholesome kind, Cyril stands under the same death sentence as his childhood friend.

Why is life so blighted in *The White Peacock*? What causes the disease and can it be cured? A tentative answer is possible but only if we stop waiting for Cyril to find it and recognize that he is actually diseased himself. Life is blighted because men and women, and the values Lawrence assigns to each sex, have been driven far apart and have no way of getting together again. The woman's value is order and form. It is associated with the home and the town. The man's value is sheer energy and animal vigor and is associated with the woodland and the farm. Women need men to invigorate and fructify the social and ethical orders they create. Men need women in order to channelize their turbulent and anarchic energies. Unfulfilled by man, woman becomes the white peacock, "all vanity and screech and defilement." Unfulfilled by woman, man gives way to the anti-social destructiveness of an Annable or the self-destructive, shapeless emotional vagaries of drunkenness.

The basic conflict of *The White Peacock*, then, is between Miranda and Caliban; and the real trouble with Cyril Beardsall as *raisonneur* is that he is too nervous ever to decide whether he wants to play Ferdinand to one or be raped by the other. Lawrence's naive, melodramatic allegory of dissociation is not such a hymn of hate against family life as *The Way of All Flesh*, finally published in the same year as Lawrence's book was finished, but it belongs with Butler's novel in celebrating the sickness of the Victorians, who gave woman a pedestal instead of enfranchising her and coarsened the subtle differences between male and female into the blighting antinomy which Lawrence's novel simultaneously accepts and deplores. In *The White Peacock* the pedestal has become the mortuary sculpture of an angel upon whose head a female bird lets fall its liquid siftings. Although the narration is vague on this point, we can imagine that the statue depicts a shy or violent male in a narcissistic pose and that the graves nearby are occupied by cock robins stricken by the hunting arrows of lady archers.

Does *The White Peacock* ever propose a remedy to the sickness it depicts? Certainly not very firmly or clearly. But if we hold in mind Lawrence's later work it becomes possible to claim that in one passing scene (pp. 128-131) a hint of future reconciliation is given. Out on a walk together, Lettie Beardsall, Leslie Tempest her fiancé, Emily, and Cyril come upon a bed of snowdrops growing in the shadow of "weird oaks tangled in the sunset." To Cyril and to Lettie also the flowers hold some meaning which people might once have been able to grasp, perhaps when the flowers were employed as ritual objects in a lost religion. Lettie remarks, "Look at them—closed up, retreating, powerless. They belong to some knowledge we have lost, that I have lost and that I need. I feel afraid." When Lettie turns to her town suitor after letting her fingers wander among the flowers, she discovers that her normal feeling for him has changed. She looks at him and laughs and says, "You do not seem real to me." A moment later, the gamekeeper looms up, like "some malicious Pan," and tries to drive the two couples away. After recognizing them he says, "Tell a woman not to come in a wood till she can look at natural things—she might see something."

The thing she might see in the wood is a man she could love without crippling, who could love her without fear. He would emerge from his dark turbulence to fructify her and she would repay the favor by showing him that energy without form is a waste of life. Unfortunately, no such wise consummation is possible in *The White Peacock*. Lawrence is still too stricken by what he has seen of the battle between feminine refinement and masculine uncouthness that raged in his own home for that. Nevertheless, this scene directly prefigures the several scenes in Lawrence's last novel, *Lady Chatterley's Lover*, in which a lady comes to a wood and lingers there until she has recovered lost knowledge that she needs. The gloomy young novelist has already created the imaginative form within which the consummation and reconciliation can take place.

3

Sons and Lovers has always been Lawrence's most popular book and will probably remain so. Stories about poor boys moving upward in life fit readily into the fantasies of self-realization indulged by all readers, especially the young. The novel is full of richly detailed specifications of place and person, it contains two female characters who are beautiful and interesting in very different ways, it is just explicit enough about physical passion to seize the imagination without inflaming it. When I first read it in adolescence I thought it very like a Hardy novel only much more luminous, and for a while I confused in my mind Miriam on her farm with Eustacia Vye beside her signal fire. Despite the claim, or perhaps to confirm the claim, that the Oedipus Complex has a universal appeal when represented in literature, I totally missed the point that Paul Morel was fixated. One knew boys just as responsive to their mothers as Paul was, and it seemed natural for him to feel very sorry when she died. Around 1939, I was probably much more interested that Paul lived in a small crowded house like mine, that when he cycled out to the countryside a pretty, intelligent girl turned up to talk and go hiking with him, that when he took a job in town he had time to paint and get to know another girl who actually slept with him.

Despite its popular appeal, which appears to be quite legitimate, *Sons and Lovers* has sometimes been charged with formlessness and with confusion of form. These two charges are usually presented as one. The first appears quite false, and so far as I know has never been substantiated. The second claim, that the novel is confused, appears more legitimate but can hardly be considered until the first has been disallowed. That is what I propose to do: to discuss how the novel is organized, and where and how a certain confusion disturbs its essential composure.

Actually, *Sons and Lovers* has three formal orders or matrices, which inhabit the same serial order of narrated words. To a degree, they blend with each other, and enrich one another. The first matrix is autobiographical narrative; the second a scheme taken over from psychoanalytic theory; the third is difficult to name because Lawrence was the first novelist to use it as a context, as opposed to a quality, of human experience, but it might be called the matrix of "life."

Each matrix has its own kind of logical articulation. The autobiographical narrative is articulated in terms of historical sequence (Mrs. Morel gave William his tea *and then* he went to the "Wakes"), and ordinary causality (Paul stopped school at the age of fourteen and went to work at Jordan's Surgical Appliance Co. *because* his family needed the money). The logic of the psychoanalytic scheme depends on a particular explanation of behavior provided by a psychological system that assumes and explains such mechanisms as unconscious motivation and projection. When the narrator says at one point about Paul's attitude toward Miriam, "He wanted now to give her passion and tenderness, and could not," it is a straightforward statement of fact according to the first matrix. But in terms of the psychological scheme it is a diagnostic description of a neurotic symptom belonging to a syndrome precisely defined by Sigmund Freud in a paper first published in 1912.

The logic of the third matrix may be termed, following Lawrence's own usage, "vital" or "passional." It is easier to show in operation than to define a priori. For example: after Mrs. Morel dies of cancer and is laid out in her bedroom, her husband Walter Morel is peculiarly reluctant to enter the room to pay his last respects. When he finally summons courage he stays only long enough to see that the body is there in the darkened room under a sheet. He does not look directly at her and see her, and in fact has not looked directly at her since the beginning of her illness. After the funeral he sits in the kitchen with her "superior" relatives and tearfully explains how he had always done his best by her. Later on, he is troubled during afternoon naps by nightmarish dreams of his dead wife which frighten him badly. According to the first matrix the sequence is ordinary. That is the way Morel is, God help him! It is still ordinary and typical according to the second matrix: the death of a close relative may precipitate an anxiety state in a survivor, and so forth. The same sequence in the vital context, where it actually takes place, leads to a severe judgment on Morel:

> And that was how he tried to dismiss her. He never
> thought of her personally. Everything deep in him he
> denied. Paul hated his father for sitting sentimentalising
> over her. He knew he would do it in the public-houses.
> For the real tragedy went on in Morel in spite of himself.
> (p. 401)

Passional or vital logic dictates this judgment. The larger indictment against the father in the novel is that he denies the life within him. Here the denial is expressed through his refusal to "see" his dead wife, and his willingness to tell sentimental lies about their relation. In the other contexts these are his experiences. In the vital context the experience violates sanctions that may be mysterious but are also specific and real. The violation is a form of self-violation and is a tragedy, according to the firm, though compassionate, view of the narration.

The three formal orders of *Sons and Lovers* can perhaps

best be illustrated by following the hero Paul Morel through the series. As the hero of an autobiographical novel Paul is a youth who grew up in a colliery village, loved and left two women, became a successful commercial artist specializing in designs for textiles, with outlets for his work in such great London stores as Liberty's, and lost a beloved mother in his mid-twenties. According to the psychological scheme, he is a classic instance of oedipal fixation. In the context of what Lawrence was soon to call in his *Study of Thomas Hardy* "the vast unexplored morality of life itself,"[4] Paul is a passionate pilgrim whose every action and impulse is a decision for or against life and accumulates to a body of fate that quite literally spells life or death for him.

The expressive means through which each of these forms is represented can be partially differentiated. The first is represented through a painstaking, richly detailed rendering of the naturalistic surface of ordinary life in both expository and dramatic terms. The psychoanalytic scheme is occasionally pointed up through explicit interpretative commentary, but is largely implicit in the autobiographical narrative as an underlying pattern. The vital context informs the naturalistic narrative, is sometimes pointed up through specific narrative comment ("For the real tragedy went on in Morel in spite of himself"), and is also expressed direct in isolable dramatic scenes of a peculiar kind and in passages of extended description that carry an intensely poetic charge. These scenes and expository passages, in which characters act out their vital destinies, sometimes mislead critics on the prowl for symbolism into supposing they were planted in the narration as "keys" to hidden meaning. But in the sense that symbols always point beyond themselves to something buried, there is little symbolism in *Sons and Lovers*. Early

---

[4] See *Phoenix: The Posthumous Papers of D. H. Lawrence*, ed. E. D. McDonald (New York: Viking, 1936), p. 418.

in the novel Miriam is shown afraid to "let herself go" fast and high when she is taking turns with Paul on the barn swing. Later on, she cannot let herself go in her sexual experiences with Paul. The first situation is not meant to adumbrate the second. Both are equally real and final as revelations of Miriam's diminished vitality, her tendency to shrink back from life, whether she is making love, feeding chickens, trying to cope with Mrs. Morel's dislike of her, or merely looking at flowers.

Not every character functions in all three matrices, although all the major characters do. Paul's younger brother Arthur, for example, has no part in the oedipal pattern, and his vitality, while evident enough, is never at issue. The elder brother William who dies at the end of Part I because he cannot resolve the conflict between his attachments to his mother and to his fiancée belongs mainly to the second matrix, as the first of Mrs. Morel's two fixated son-lovers. Miss Limb, the lonely farm woman in love with the stallion, who appears briefly in Chapter IX: "The Defeat of Miriam," belongs mainly to the third context. Lawrence is interested, not in her psychology or her personal history, but solely in her rapport with the animal as that rapport affects Paul, Miriam, and Clara. Their reactions to her define qualities of being each possesses and clarify the continually modified emotional currents passing among the three young people, constituting their relation at that particular time.

Now that the form of *Sons and Lovers* has been defined, it becomes possible to deal with the charge of formal confusion. Confusion arises owing to a final inescapable conflict between the psychoanalytic and the vital contexts. Each approaches experience from a somewhat different angle, interprets it differently, and posits a different sort of hero. Paul is finally caught in a dual focus. As a case study of neurosis he is trapped in a pattern of "repetition compulsion" from which there is no escape this side of the analyst's couch. He therefore seems to be left at the end in the "drift toward death" mentioned in Lawrence's Freudian summary of the novel which he sent in a letter to Edward Garnett.[5] As a "vital" hero Paul, although threatened with death, owing to the sheer difficulty of the human relationships he has thrust upon him in childhood and develops on his own in early manhood, has a better than even chance of maintaining himself whole and alive in the midst of life as the novel ends.

The conflict, with its attendant ambiguities which confuse the presentation of Miriam and Clara as well as Paul, is real but ought not to be exaggerated, as it has been by critics whose notions of formal coherence are narrowly based. Psychoanalysis and Lawrence's kind of vitalism have many points in common as readings of experience. There is a sense in which the "drift toward death" means as much in passional as in neurotic terms. But the two systems of interpretation finally do not coincide. The Freudian system is weighted toward determinism. Paul, given his conditioning and the axiom that unconscious processes cannot become conscious and therefore modifiable without a therapist's aid, is doomed. The vital context is a fluid system that is fully indeterminate. Short of death there is no occasion in experience when the individual cannot make the correct, life-enhancing choice. Even an old wreck like Morel *could* at last look at his dead wife—the possibility is implied by the very strictness with which his refusal to do so is judged. The issues of life and death are fully worked into the very texture of events, and the road to salvation runs along the edge

[5] See *The Letters of D. H. Lawrence*, ed. A. Huxley (New York: Viking, 1932), pp. 78-79. Hereafter cited as *Letters*.

of the abyss where Paul stands after his mother's death and his double rejection of Clara and Miriam.

Although both novels draw upon the same set of remembered facts, *Sons and Lovers* is infinitely superior to *The White Peacock* as an autobiographical narrative. The latter totally suppresses the industrial milieu, arbitrarily raises the social level of the Beardsall family from working class to shabby-genteel, substitutes preposterous scenes of upper-class "society" at a manor house called Highclose for the domestic routines of a miner's household. Cyril, who is quite obviously an early study for Paul Morel, is also quite obviously in love with his mother. That is really why he is so half-hearted in his spasmodic search for adult love and relatedness. But except for a few brief indications, this crucial relationship is missing from the book. In Cyril, we get the burden of sick feeling without its referent—a devouring maternal possessiveness which destroys a son's capacity to move on from childhood attachments into adulthood.

Sons and Lovers not only confronts the mother-son relation directly but places it at the center of a real world built up through an astonishingly detailed recreation of a complex human environment. In the early chapters the mother's shift of her affections from her husband to her sons is sketched against a background that includes the social and economic history of the Nottinghamshire-Derbyshire border region going back nearly two centuries, includes two earlier generations of family history, an exhaustive account of the social structure of a colliery village, a description of the patterns of work and recreation of the men who dig the coal and their wives who toil behind the weathered brick façades of the row houses on the valley's southern slope. When Paul begins to visit the Leivers' farm the exposition broadens to include full descriptions of the countryside, which contrasts so finally and suggestively with the grimy village, and of Miriam's entire family, how they came to the farm and how they work it. When he takes a job in Nottingham the exposition broadens again. We come to understand the exact routines of a small Victorian factory, and its human environment as well. And we learn of the surrounding city, with its great grey castle, swift river, hurtling trams, and enormous mills.

This background is deeply relevant to the central conflicts of the book. It conditions the struggle of some of the characters to realize themselves and helps explain the baffled compromise that other characters make with the circumstances into which they were born. I know of no other English novel, with the possible exception of George Eliot's *Middlemarch*, where people are so rooted in concrete social history, and in a region so concretely rendered. It becomes possible to measure the precise degree of freedom or unfreedom enjoyed by each major character in relation to the full human environment.

It is worth spelling some of this out. Gertrude Morel's incompatibility with her husband is conditioned by particular social facts. Her father had been a Nottingham lace manufacturer ruined by an industrial slump. She marries beneath her partly because she has lost her marriage portion, partly because a tentative engagement to a scholarly young man has fallen through. When she comes to the village of Bestwood to live with Morel she leaves a large city in touch with the great world for a narrow, spiritually and economically impoverished mining community dominated by traditional codes affecting all areas of life from child care to the manner in which a collier divides his time, and money, between the pub and the home. She tries to adapt herself, but is soon put off by the uncouth slackness of her husband. Yet his qualities are also conditioned by social facts. His fecklessness is in tune with the community as a whole. The village has changed little in several generations and now faces a diminishing basis of economic support as the long worked coal veins yield an ever narrowing margin of profit. Morel went into the pits at twelve. The warm physical nature which had attracted Gertrude to him is soon ruined by hard work, by serious accidents occurring in the pit at regular intervals, and by drink. The rupture between husband and wife, although inevitable, is never total. In the midst of her contempt she respects what he once was; and Morel's drunken tirades hide an inarticulate admiration for her real refinement and intellectual superiority.

Still, it is equally inevitable that she should turn to her sons as they mature toward manhood. They become the channels into which she pours her long dammed up spiritual energy, and she cannot help using them destructively to break a way through the walls separating her from a larger world. The older son is taken over completely. He wears himself out in ambitious pursuits reflecting an intensity of frustration that is more his mother's than his own. Denied its legitimate satisfactions, Mrs. Morel's will has become inhuman. Paul, with some of the traditional slipperiness of the artist type, evades the full force of the mother's will, but is severely injured by the erotic concomitants of her drive for self-realization through a son's life. At the same time, both sons' choices are closely circumscribed by social facts. They can follow the father into the pit—while fully idiomatic, the expression has a peculiar ring in the context of Bestwood's chapel-going religiosity—or side with their mother in favor of culture, education, and money. The terms in which the choice is posed are preposterously unfair, but they are dictated by prevailing social arrangements, not by the whim of either working-class parent.

The same sort of conditioning operates on characters

other than the Morels. Miriam's frigid attitude toward sex and her masochistic, compensatory version of Christian belief comes to her from her mother, a town woman of rather low physical vigor forced to live on a small tenant farm where all must work to the point of exhaustion if the rent is to be cleared each year. Exhausted by her work and child-bearing, repelled by the spectacle of farm animals in heat or giving birth, Mrs. Leivers recoils from the sex relation and solaces herself with chapel religion. Clara Dawes's poignant blend of hauteur and humility, as well as her bitter quarrel with Baxter, reflects the conflict between her aspirations and her circumstances. She wants freedom to become someone, but is only free to choose between the factory and a damaged marriage to an ordinary workman. As a suffragette she blames her troubles on the unfranchised status of women, yet the novel makes clear that her lot is the same as her husband's and like poor people's generally.

Lawrence's translation of socioeconomic abstractions into terms of human actuality is thorough. A broken love affair, a family quarrel, Mrs. Morel's anxiety upon entering Lincoln Cathedral lest she be asked to leave because her clothes are not fine enough, are, conversely, events belonging to history. One wonders where there is any margin of freedom left the characters. But the novel insists on this margin of freedom. Mrs. Morel should not have dehumanized her will. Morel should not have hidden his injured feelings behind a shell of brutal cynicism. Miriam should have found the courage to take Paul in the novel's penultimate scene when he was there for the taking. Clara must find the strength and forbearance to re-create her marriage with Dawes. Failure to do these things may fulfill a tragic pattern in history, but it violates the vital sanctions I mentioned earlier. Beyond the close circumscriptions of social fact life goes on. It is the farther context within which human history is placed, as the village, or the city or the lonely farm is set down within wild nature. The individual is rooted in life as well as history and cannot escape his own freedom to make the choices that life will judge by an inscrutable morality.

Paul Morel is the proper hero of *Sons and Lovers* because he holds and uses this freedom in a greater measure than any other character. He imposes himself. In calling the book an autobiographical narrative I do not mean that it is a faithful reproduction of Lawrence's career up to the time his mother died. Recollected material has been re-organized and new material has been added to make a dramatic pattern emphasizing Paul's dominating character. Paul's vitality is stronger, his awareness of vital issues is finer than Lawrence's. The paradox is only apparent and can easily be sustained. In life Lawrence was baffled by Jessie Chambers, whose indignant assertion that they never became lovers compels belief. Lawrence was initiated into sex by a Mrs. Dax. She took him upstairs one afternoon because she thought he needed it. As a boy he worked for a surgical appliance company like Jordan's but left after only a few weeks because the factory girls jeered at him and one day removed his trousers in a dark corner of one of the storerooms.

In *Sons and Lovers* Paul forces his agonized relation with Miriam to the final issue of sexual union and then leaves her only when he is satisfied that they are too much at emotional cross-purposes to marry. He is entirely dominant in the affair with Clara, even to the point of forcing a reconciliation between Baxter and Clara before withdrawing into a *nuit blanche* of grief over his mother's death. He enjoys his work in the factory, develops affectionate ties with the girls who work there, and after several years has so thoroughly shaped the routines of his job to his own needs that he manages to spend only the mornings as a spiral clerk, using his afternoons to paint in a spare room. Finally, he copes with his mother during her illness. After speaking the ghastly sentence, "It is the living I want, not the dead," Mrs. Morel has fixed her will on survival even though she has a metastasized cancer and is in monstrous pain. Paul's decision to perform a mercy killing is simultaneously an act of the purest love, and a victory over the maternal will which guarantees that at the end he will find a way to escape the "drift toward death" which follows her death. It is also a free decision to take a constructive line of action against the destructiveness implicit in Mrs. Morel's will to survive after any real life has left her.

There is no point in saying that Paul's career merely compensates for Lawrence's career, that he is a fantasy dreamed up by Cyril Beardsall during one of his broods on Nethermere shore. Certainly Paul is bigger and freer than the young Lawrence, but he is not freer and bigger than Lawrence's vision of what life can be. Nevertheless it is mainly because Paul is a hero rather than a victim in the context of autobiographical narrative that Lawrence's employment of the psychoanalytic scheme works at cross purposes with the other matrices.

It will be useful here to summarize Lawrence's relation to Freud with particular reference to the period in which he was composing *Sons and Lovers*.[6] We do not know whether Lawrence had read Freud before he wrote the final draft of *Sons and Lovers*, but it is definitely known that Frieda had read Freud and discussed psychoanalytic

[6] The most informed discussions of this problem are to be found in Frederick J. Hoffman's *Freudianism and the Literary Mind* (Baton Rouge, Louisiana: Louisiana State University Press, 1945), pp. 149-180, and in the first edition of *The Intelligent Heart* (New York: Farrar Straus & Young, 1954), pp. 131-132.

ideas with Lawrence on numerous occasions while he worked on the final draft of the novel. Lawrence's first contact with professional analysts did not come until 1914, when he made the acquaintance of Dr. David Eder and Barbara Low. In Lawrence's later writings he frequently took issue with the Freudians on two points: on the primacy of the sexual impulse in the individual's psychological development; on the value of bringing neurotics to a conscious awareness of repressed instincts and drives. Since one of the principal stresses in his entire career was his attack on the modern tendency to overconceptualize experience, it was inevitable that he should come to take issue with the Freudian school.

It remains to determine the accuracy of Lawrence's representation of the Oedipus complex from the Freudian standpoint. Without claiming expertness in these matters I should say that Lawrence's construction of a sort of neurotic case history for Paul is both accurate and comprehensive. *Sons and Lovers* presents the mother fixation, the abnormal jealousy of the father, and shows both these tendencies persisting as a disturbing influence in Paul's dealings with men and women outside the family circle; for instance, the affair with Clara, which is broken off as the result of a savage fight between Paul and the jealous husband, represents on one level an acting out of an oedipal fantasy wherein Clara and Baxter Dawes, the estranged and quarrelsome married couple, replace Gertrude and Walter Morel, the hero's own mother and father. Furthermore, the novel dramatizes the conflict in the hero between normal desires and unconscious fixations. It presents his ambivalence —his oscillations between love and hate in the affair with Miriam—and it dramatizes the mechanism of projection whereby Paul transfers his internal conflicts to the outside world.

One further point. The psychological theme of the "split" which Lawrence develops both within the novel and also in the letter to Edward Garnett mentioned earlier is actually the same as that developed by Sigmund Freud in his essay, "The Most Prevalent Form of Degradation in Erotic Life."[7] Here is described a widespread condition of psychical impotence in modern, cultivated men in which individuals, because of an unresolved incestuous attachment for their mothers, combined with an unusually repressed childhood and adolescence, find it impossible to fuse tender and sensual feelings into a wholesome love for a woman of their own age and station in life. These men are sexually attracted by women who are in some way inferior to them, while the tenderness they feel for their feminine social equals lacks a sensual quality. They give their souls to women who play the role of mother figures and their bodies to women who for one reason or another can never aspire to represent the over-idealized mother.

Thus as Lawrence wrote to Garnett, William Morel "gives his sex to a fribble, and his mother holds his soul." Paul seems to do better by consummating his love for the companionable Miriam. But his constant complaints that she is too soulful and that she is frigid, alike with the death urges he frequently experiences after intercourse with her, show that he cannot heal the split in his affective life through Miriam. Later on he divides his love between the idealized mother and the passionate, shamed, compromised Clara Dawes. In classical neurotic fashion he re-creates again and again the very conditions of unhealth from which he is attempting to escape.

Paul's vitality, his extraordinary capacity to make boldly

[7] Freud's essay appears in English translation by Joan Riviere in the *Collected Papers* (London: Hogarth Press, 1953), IV, 203-216.

sensuous responses to his environment, suggest that he is somehow free. The above summary of the facts of his "case" show that he is not. This difference cannot be compromised. It represents a collision between opposed ways of looking at a character, opposed definitions of human instinct and of human fate. One summer evening, after Paul has been sleeping with Miriam for an entire year, he steps suddenly out of doors:

> The beauty of the night made him want to shout. A half-moon, dusky gold, was sinking behind the black sycamore at the end of the garden, making the sky dull purple with its glow. Nearer, a dim white fence of lilies went across the garden, and the air all round seemed to stir with scent, as if it were alive. He went across the bed of pinks, whose keen perfume came sharply across the rocking, heavy scent of the lilies, and stood alongside the white barrier of flowers. They flagged all loose, as if they were panting. The scent made him drunk. He went down to the field to watch the moon sink under.
>
> A corncrake in the hay-close called insistently. The moon slid quite quickly downwards, growing more flushed. Behind him the great flowers leaned as if they were calling. And then, like a shock, he caught another perfume, something raw and coarse. Hunting round, he found the purple iris, touched their fleshy throats and their dark, grasping hands. At any rate, he had found something. They stood stiff in the darkness. Their scent was brutal. The moon was melting down upon the crest of the hill. It was gone; all was dark. The corncrake called still.
>
> Breaking off a pink, he suddenly went indoors.
>
> "Come, my boy," said his mother. "I'm sure it's time you went to bed."
>
> He stood with the pink against his lips.
>
> "I shall break off with Miriam, mother," he answered calmly.　　(pp. 293-294)

After noting that the raw coarse scent of the iris evokes Clara, as the pinks whose petals he soon spits into the fire evoke Miriam; after noting the presence of the mother and her characteristically domineering mode of address, one must still insist that the decision springs to life out of Paul's fully concrete experience of the night, the garden and the flowers in their nearly overpowering physical actuality. We may find the hero's relation to these a mystery and his decision brutal, but we have to admit that the experience is *sui generis*, not simply another instance of Paul's enslavement to what Freud called, rather abstractedly, an *imago*. Scenes of this type suggest that beneath the layer of disordered instinctual trends constituting Paul's neurosis lie other vital impulses which remain intact and occasionally break through, with a consequent shock of recognition for both the reader and the character. Paul is tied but carries his freedom somewhere inside him, whence it might issue, given the appropriate challenge from the life teeming around him, here represented by a beautiful summer night, to dissolve his bonds and transform his existence.

Thus when Paul goes to Miriam to announce that their love affair is over he is everything despicable that she thinks he is: chiefly, "an infant which, when it has drunk its fill, throws away and smashes the cup" in the name of an illusory freedom. But while she sits there, having seen through him—

> His very movements fascinated her as if she were hypnotized by him. Yet he was despicable, false, inconsistent, and mean. . . . Why was it the movement of his arm stirred her as nothing else in the world could? (p. 298)

The answer is evident enough. She is stirred by "the movement of active life," by the "quickness" that is imprisoned in him, for which she loves him, yet which neither she nor any other woman, least of all the mother, knows how to release.

The ending of *Sons and Lovers* shows that Paul Morel's nature does contain an intact core of vitality which is his freedom, that while his responses to his family and mistresses have been "overdetermined" by neuroticism, his fate remains indeterminate *au fond*. When Mrs. Morel is dead, the hero cries out, "My love—my love—oh, my love!" echoing the cry of the mother—"My son, oh my son"—over the body of William. But for Paul there is no one to turn to, no one to build a new life upon, and he turns away into his white night of spiritual and emotional numbness. He puts his affairs in order by reconciling Clara with Baxter and goes alone to encounter his self-annihilating vision of the voidness of a world which no longer contains his mother. Darkness washes over him in a great flood. It pours from the infinite reaches of space, and wells up from inside, "from his breast, from his mouth." It is a flood of dissolution:

> When he turned away he felt the last hold for him had gone. The town, as he sat upon the car, stretched away over the bay of railway, a level fume of lights. Beyond the town the country, little smouldering spots for more towns—the sea—the night—on and on! And he had no place in it! Whatever spot he stood on, there he stood alone. From his breast, from his mouth, sprang the endless space, and it was there behind him, everywhere. The people hurrying along the streets offered no obstruction to the void in which he found himself. They were small shadows whose footsteps and voices could be heard, but in each of them the same night, the same silence. He got off the car. In the country all was dead still. Little stars shone high up; little stars spread far away in the flood-waters, a firmament below. Everywhere the vastness and terror of the immense night

THE DEED OF LIFE

which is roused and stirred for a brief while by the day, but
which returns, and will remain at last eternal, holding
everything in its silence and its living gloom. There was no
Time, only Space. Who could say his mother had lived
and did not live? She had been in one place, and was in
another; that was all. And his soul could not leave her,
wherever she was. Now she was gone abroad into the
night, and he was with her still. They were together.
But yet there was his body, his chest, that leaned against
the stile, his hands on the wooden bar. They seemed something. Where was he?—one tiny upright speck of flesh, less
than an ear of wheat lost in the field. He could not bear it.
On every side the immense dark silence seemed pressing
him, so tiny a spark, into extinction, and yet, almost nothing,
he could not be extinct. Night, in which everything was
lost, went reaching out, beyond stars and sun. Stars and sun,
a few bright grains, went spinning round for terror, and
holding each other in embrace, there in a darkness that
outpassed them all, and left them tiny and daunted. So
much, and himself, infinitesimal, at the core a nothingness,
and yet not nothing.   (pp. 419-420)

"After such knowledge what forgiveness?" The hero
stands on the brink of disintegration, a nothingness, "and
yet not nothing." It is clear from the passage that if he is
somehow to be saved he has only the stubborn physical fact
of his own body and its mysterious life with which to resist
the night. The pressure of his body leaning against the stile
effectively prevents him from moving toward death and
the mother. And in the comparison of the body to an "ear
of wheat" there is the faintest suggestion of a germinating
potential out of which may spring forth the opportunity
of renewal. There is not the slightest indication that escape
from self-disintegration will be easy or assured. The movement toward the city's "gold phosphorescence" does not
contradict, as some critics have thought, the drift toward
death of which Lawrence's thematic summary speaks. A

physical body is set in motion toward the "humming, glowing town," but it is clear from the whole tendency of the novel, clear also from Paul's envisionment of stars and sun as "a few bright grains . . . spinning round for terror," that the tiny glow of the town lights up no safe harbor.

Paul Morel at the end is of necessity and by virtue of his own free act released from the maternal bondage which, if long continued, would have destroyed him. But this freedom involves alienation and isolation from the world. As he moves toward the urban settlement which Lawrence describes in his *Study of Thomas Hardy* as "the little fold of law and order, the little walled city within which man has to defend himself against the waste enormity of nature,"[8] it is possible to see the hero embarking on a quest after health and relatedness. For the dramatization of such a quest, the reader must turn to the later novels.

Here it is enough to attempt some definition of the stance of the vital hero, vis-à-vis the world, since Paul is assuredly the first hero of Lawrence's fiction who can be so called. He faces life with the knowledge that no theological sanctions exist to make its burdens tolerable; that life itself represents the faintest glimmer of warmth within the cold, infinite reaches of dead space; that human life in its various social, economic, and personal orders is filled with destructive forces; that his own integrity is blighted by the conditioning to which he has been exposed. In the face of this knowledge he accepts freely his responsibility for action in conformity with an instinctive morality of life which is largely inscrutable yet by which he will be mercilessly judged. The stance may be considered quixotic, but not unheroic, especially when compared with the postures of neo-orthodoxy, metaphysical rebellion, or bland indifference which have been assumed by various sorts of gifted people in this century.

[8] See *Phoenix*, p. 419.

PART II

THE DISCOVERY OF FORM

THE RAINBOW
WOMEN IN LOVE

1

WHEN novelists introduce remarks about another art form into a book, there is usually ground for suspicion that they are commenting obliquely on their own, specifically literary intentions. Paul Morel, although only a part-time painter, has rather definite ideas of what he is after. One day when Miriam is admiring one of his sketches, he explains confidently that it is good

> because there is scarcely any shadow in it; it's more shimmery, as if I'd painted the shimmering protoplasm in the leaves and everywhere, and not the stiffness of the shape. That seems dead to me. Only this shimmeriness is the real living. The shape is a dead crust. The shimmer is inside really.   (p. 152)

And after several years have passed it is said of him that

> he loved to paint large figures, full of light, but not merely made up of lights and cast shadows, like the impressionists; rather definite figures that had a certain luminous quality, like some of Michael Angelo's people. And these he fitted into a landscape in what he thought true proportion. He worked a great deal from memory, using everybody he knew.   (p. 301)

Painting the shimmer and the effort to render "a certain luminous quality" would seem to correspond with Lawrence's effort to depict the inner vitality of Paul's nature, or of a landscape, as discussed in the last chapter; just as the reference to working from memory evokes the autobiographical framework of *Sons and Lovers*. But there are some difficulties in this miniature aesthetic theory, whether it is applied to painting or to fiction. For instance, it would seem impossible to paint the protoplasmic inscape of the

35

leaves direct. If the shape is a dead crust it is still the only vehicle by means of which the "real living" that is inside shows forth, unless the painter abandons representation altogether and tries to re-create the shimmer through some sort of abstract technique. But one feels that both Paul and his creator are too much in love with the phenomenal world to follow in the footsteps of a Kandinsky or a Jackson Pollock. The second passage actually seems to be a compromise of the position stated in the first. Here Paul commits himself to definiteness of representation, but tries to imbue his figures with a luminousness that will suggest indirectly the energies inside.

Nevertheless, as Lawrence always insisted, modes of construing reality in art inevitably demonstrate the values by which the artist lives. And Paul, only a few pages after his solution of his problems as a painter, shows that he is far from satisfied with the same compromise as a human being. He is in the first flood of his passion for Clara and must wait through an entire working day at the factory before he can be alone with her. His tension mounts, and the last quarter hour before they meet is sheer torture. He reflects, or Lawrence reflects for him, "It was the anguish of combining the living self with the shell." At this point the living self is Paul's powerful urge to be with Clara; the shell is routine, work, ultimately the sum of complex social and economic arrangements that prevent action on a basis of pure spontaneity. The shell is also part of Paul. He wills himself to work, to wait, to suppress the impulse to go immediately to Clara; he forces himself to act in a civilized manner. His human dignity and his sanity entail this "anguish of combining"; for were he to act altogether spontaneously, altogether protoplasmically, he would end on the gallows or in a madhouse in short order.

What of Paul's theory of art as a theory of fiction? The

same problems crop up and the same solution suggests it-self. The novel, inasmuch as it portrays society, and men and women who belong ineluctably to society as well as to themselves, is even more strongly involved with the crust and the shell than painting. The problem of fitting luminous figures into a landscape in true proportion is simpler than the novelist's problem of representing living selves, par-ticularly when the "real living" is inside, in combination with the stiff shapes of an industrial society, especially when part of the stiffness must attach itself to the individual character and not simply to the social arrangements sur-rounding him. Thus, Walter Morel by late middle age is all shell. The mine, and the town, and the pub have de-troyed the life inside him in exactly the same way as suc-cessive layers of heavy armor would crush and suffocate a living body beneath.

At the end of *Sons and Lovers* Paul Morel, a minute shimmer of vitality, turns away from the void toward so-ciety. He faces a new anguish of combining. If he fails he will end like his father, his livingness snuffed out. If he succeeds—if there is a real merging of Paul's livingness with the forms of society—not only will he realize his vital self but the form of society will be to a certain extent trans-formed. The stiffness of the societal crust will give way. The forms of social existence will take on a certain luminous quality.

If one imagines that Paul went on to become a novelist, one would assume that he would try to bring about a con-frontation between his sense of life and his hard-won, tragic understanding of how deadness inheres in socioeconomic processes and in the experiences of people tied to each other as a nation, a community, a family, as lovers and as friends. His books would attempt to show how human freedom, defined as a real livingness within the person, can be released to crack the dead crust of industrial society and build society anew. This would be his special "anguish of combining," and would be exacerbated by his recognition that society is increasingly organized for death, as shown in the recurrent cataclysms of global war and the spread of the abstracted systems of industrial production and distribution. He would be tempted in this anguish, as he was tempted while waiting for Clara, to abandon himself to pure spontaneity or to the pastoral simplifications suggested by figures in a landscape in true proportions. But his honesty, and his loyalty to the medium of fiction, with its inescapable commitment to the representation of man in society, as well as its utter incapacity to portray spontaneity against a void, would bring him back to his main task.

Paul's hypothetical problems are, of course, Lawrence's life-long problems as a novelist who sought to put his ideas of freedom at the service of a sick society, and sometimes recoiled from the anguish of combining this enterprise demanded. Lawrence, immediately after finishing *Sons and Lovers*, recoiled briefly in a fashion that must be analyzed before going on to consider his achievement in *The Rainbow*. Evidence of this recoil is contained in a remarkable letter to Edward Garnett[1] which clarified his intentions with respect to *The Rainbow* after Garnett had responded unfavorably to an early draft of that book. Because it is of central importance for an understanding of the direction Lawrence's creative thought took after *Sons and Lovers* it must be quoted at length:

> I don't think the psychology is wrong: it is only that I
> have a different attitude to my characters, and that necessitates a different attitude in you, which you are not

[1] 5 June 1914. *Letters*, pp. 199-201.

prepared to give. As for its being my *cleverness* which would pull the thing through—that sounds odd to me, for I don't think I am so very clever, in that way. I think the book is a bit futuristic—quite unconsciously so. But when I read Marinetti—"the profound intuitions of life added one to the other, word by word, according to their illogical conception, will give us the general lines of an intuitive physiology of matter"—I see something of what I am after. I translate him clumsily, and his Italian is obfuscated—and I don't care about physiology of matter—but somehow—that which is physic—non-human, in humanity, is more interesting to me than the old-fashioned human element—which causes one to conceive a character in a certain moral scheme and make him consistent. The certain moral scheme is what I object to. In Turgenev, and in Tolstoi, and in Dostoievsky, the moral scheme into which all the characters fit—and it is nearly the same scheme—is, whatever the extraordinariness of the characters themselves, dull, old, dead. When Marinetti writes: "It is the solidity of a blade of steel that is interesting by itself, that is, the incomprehending and inhuman alliance of its molecules in resistance to, let us say, a bullet. The heat of a piece of wood or iron is in fact more passionate, for us, than the laughter or tears of a woman"—then I know what he means. He is stupid, as an artist, for contrasting the heat of the iron and the laugh of the woman. Because what is interesting in the laugh of the woman is the same as the binding of the molecules of steel or their action in heat: it is the inhuman will, call it physiology, or like Marinetti—physiology of matter, that fascinates me. I don't so much care about what the woman *feels*—in the ordinary usage of the word. That presumes an *ego* to feel with. I only care about what the woman *is*—what she IS—inhumanly, physiologically, materially—according to the use of the word: but for me, what she *is* as a phenomenon (or as representing some greater, inhuman will), instead of what she feels according to the human conception. That is where the futurists are stupid. Instead of looking for the new human phenomenon, they will only look for the phenomena of the science of physics to be found in human beings. They are crassly stupid. But if anyone would give them eyes, they would pull the right apples off the tree, for their stomachs are true in appetite. You mustn't look in my novel for the old stable ego of the character. There is another ego, according to whose action the individual is unrecognizable, and passes through, as it were allotropic states which it needs a deeper sense than any we've been used to exercise to discover are states of the same single radically-unchanged element. (Like as diamond and coal are the same pure single element of carbon. The ordinary novel would trace the history of the diamond—but I say, "Diamond, what! This is carbon." And my diamond might be coal or soot, and my theme is carbon.) You must not say my novel is shaky —it is not perfect, because I am not expert in what I want to do. But it is the real thing, say what you like. And I shall get my reception, if not now, then before long. Again I say, don't look for the development of the novel to follow the lines of certain characters: the characters fall into the form of some other rhythmic form, as when one draws a fiddlebow across a fine tray delicately sanded, the sand takes lines unknown.

In this program for art Lawrence's concern for the core of vitality in the human self, which defines its basic integrity and freedom, has been translated into an attack on traditional ideas of character and plot which were serviceable once but have come to reflect the stiffness and deadness of a society gone wrong. As an artist interested in "profound intuitions of life," and in inhuman elements of the human person, which together imply a radical revision of traditional moral ideas, he cannot afford to waste time on the portrayal of individuals possessing a conventional social, moral, and psychological character within a "certain moral scheme." In the ordinary novel an individual is revealed solely by what he says, does, thinks, and feels in the context of an action and in the context of history and society. But a novelist obsessed with "isness," with an ultimate of being, must find such superficial levels of human function irrelevant to his main task. The physiological metaphors used in the letter, and the quotations from Marinetti, show that the ultimate beings of the characters must be located in the depths of the physical self. When Lawrence speaks of caring only for "what the woman *is* inhumanly, physiologically, materially . . . what she is as a phenomenon (or as representing some greater, inhuman will)" he is proposing as it were to make a force of life the hero of a novel and to show that force in action upon and through the physical substance of the individual character. He will show how life lives a woman and a man at the deepest levels, and in the process will reveal for the first time what a character *is* rather than merely what he does.

The difficulty with these ideas as they apply to any novel —although the same difficulties might not present themselves in a ballet, musical composition, or painting concerned with ultimates of being—should be obvious. In all narrative art, existence must grapple with and help to define essence; or, in other words, if one cares to differentiate characters from one another—and upon the possibility of such differentiation depends the possibility of dramatic and narrative organization—it must be done in terms of what they say, do, think, and feel humanly and socially, and these terms must mediate what they "inhumanly" are. A representation of sheer "isness" would make it impossible to distinguish one character from another, and all the characters from undifferentiated life itself. If the essence of a character is carbon, then the essence of all characters is carbon, and you cannot write a novel about carbon and nothing but carbon.

Nevertheless, as soon as we turn from the letter to *The Rainbow* itself we see that the novel is fundamentally an enterprise of combining rather than a despairing recoil. For each major character Lawrence creates two distinct selves, the self of ordinary social and familial experience involved in daily events and aiming at limited goals, and the self of essential being involved in mysterious transactions with the "living universe" and aiming at a goal unknown. He tries to show that the most valuable human enterprise is the dual fulfillment of the social and the inhuman selves within a single integrated experience of life, and at the end envisions the transformation of society into a new form within which just such saving fulfillments could work themselves out. The rainbow metaphor comes to stand for many things before the novel is finished, but finally it stands for the possibility of reconciliation between the vital self and the human community.

The theme of *The Rainbow*[2] is not carbon but salvation. The book is an attempt to show that the events and encounters of common life are charged with a life-giving, transforming potential, charged negatively also with the

<hr />

[2] After passing through eight major manuscript revisions *The Rainbow* was published on September 30, 1915, and suppressed on grounds of obscenity by court proceedings in November of the same year. In a letter to Lady Ottoline Morrell, written on July 9, 1915, Lawrence had described the novel as "the voyage of discovery towards the real and eternal and unknown land" (*Letters*, p. 244).

power of death. Salvation does not refer to heavenly rewards but to a wholesome state of being attainable here and
now. This condition can be reached only in relation with
another person. The crucial relation in *The Rainbow* is between a man and a woman in marital and sexual experience.

Throughout the novel Lawrence holds out the goal of
"transfiguration" for the various characters who seek fulfillment in their lives. Although every important character
is involved at one time or another in a desperate quest after
this fulfillment, no character experiences transfiguration
following conscious pursuit of this elusive ideal. Life selects
an Ursula Brangwen for salvation, while it dismisses her
fiancé, Anton Skrebensky, to perdition. No ordinary principle of justice is involved and certainly no principle of
mercy. Salvation issues as a call from the "unknown," and
many seek but few are called. The most that any character
can do is recognize the call when it issues from some inscrutable heart of life which can neither be named nor cog-
nitively known. The call is not from God, but the religious
imagery and symbolism with which the narration is satu-
rated constantly suggest that the mysterious transactions of
the characters with obscure vital forces are susceptible of a
religious interpretation.

What are the central values the novel embodies which
give a meaning to its idea of salvation? The famous passage of description on the opening pages answers this question. Here two orientations toward life are described, one
consisting of a mindless union with organic creation called
"blood-intimacy," the other consisting of a capacity for a
"higher form of being," for a career marked by individual
moral effort, intelligent awareness, and spiritual power.
Initially, we are told that it was the earlier generations of
Brangwen men who enjoyed the inarticulate contentment
of blood-intimacy, while their wives were concerned with

"higher being." But it is made clear in the ensuing narrative of three recent generations of Brangwens that neither of these orientations is sufficient by itself. Each represents an essential value, but wholeness of being exists only when the two values—we may call one the value of spontaneous relatedness, the other the value of maximum individuation —are brought together in a single, organized experience of life.

So far we might surmise that the two values are permanently associated with the masculine and feminine principles, as they were implicitly in *The White Peacock* and *Sons and Lovers*, and that they can be joined together only when a man takes a woman in matrimony. (Marriage is of course the major recurring event in *The Rainbow*.) But this is not the case. The mystical theory of marriage preached by the drunken Tom Brangwen in Chapter V: "Wedding at the Marsh"—"What I say is, that when a man's soul and a woman's soul unites together—that makes an Angel"—may imply that marriage by itself assures wholeness; but an earlier, soberer description of marriage modifies this idea. In the first chapter the relation of Alfred Brangwen and his unnamed wife is described as follows:

> They were two very separate beings, vitally connected,
> knowing nothing of each other, yet living in their
> separate ways from one root.   (p. 8)

From this description a reader can surmise that blood-intimacy is realized in the physical bond between the married couple, while the value of individuation is fulfilled for each in "separate ways"; that is, in the distinct pursuits which occupy their daytime existence as social beings.

The principal characters obey then—or fail to obey— a double imperative. They are impelled to seek unison with the life pulsating outside themselves through the sexual consummation primary to marriage, and simultaneously they have the responsibility to forge for themselves an individuality which will not only incorporate the higher spiritual impulses of human consciousness but also represent their adaptation to the world of society and industry. It should surprise no one that this second imperative has both an ideal and a purely practical side. The evidence is spread through many of Lawrence's writings that he regarded work as, in some sense, a spiritual activity.[3] Day labor, whether humble, professional, or artistic, provides opportunities for self-development. In *The Rainbow* Will Brangwen's temporary withdrawal of interest from his profession into total absorption with the sensuous pleasures of his wedded state is presented as evidence of a serious flaw in his character.

At the same time, given this attitude toward work, Lawrence is concerned to point out those forms of industrial organization which, because of their efficient reduction of complex craft activities to simple, repetitive actions, dehumanize work and the worker. If *The Rainbow* has a hell it is described in Chapter XII: "Shame." The new mining town of Wiggiston with its great "mathematical colliery" designed to depersonalize the working relationships of its laborers, with its spectacle of gaunt miners moving along asphalt pavements "not like living people, but like spectres," with its quality of "chaos perpetuated, persisting, chaos fixed and rigid," is an inferno of the modern mechanistic spirit. If it is to be roofed and barred against entry for future generations, a new redemption of mankind will be necessary. In this novel the redeeming possibility is equated to the values determining a perfected life—maxi-

---

[3] *Study of Thomas Hardy* again supplies a useful reference. See especially Chapters I-V in *Phoenix*, pp. 398-440.

mum relatedness in mysterious association with maximum individuation.

I have called these values imperatives and it will be readily seen that they involve conflict. A character who seeks unison with life and simultaneously a personal form of differentiation must move in two different moral directions at once. Lawrence was well aware of the conflict and took joy in it. In an essay called "The Crown,"[4] written shortly after the novel, he provided a kind of doctrinal commentary on themes dramatized in *The Rainbow*. All life is a warring of opposites, of flesh and spirit, emotion and reason, organic instinct and spiritual insight. This war is symbolized in the essay by the traditional figures of the lion and the unicorn who contend for the crown. For Lawrence the crown of their contention is wholeness of being, and he is careful to state repeatedly that this crown is the contention itself, and not some third thing in which all opposites become reconciled:

> And there is no rest, no cessation from the conflict. For we are two opposites which exist by virtue of our opposition. Remove the opposition and there is a collapse, a sudden crumbling into universal nothingness.

The characters of *The Rainbow* live in an extraordinary state of tension, both within themselves and through their connections with others. As the above quotation shows, the tension is essential to their living experience and not by itself a sign of any shortcoming.

Lawrence presents his scheme of salvation in three major episodes dealing with three successive generations of a sin-

---

[4] The essay is contained in three issues of a short-lived magazine, *The Signature*, edited by J. Middleton Murry and Katherine Mansfield and published in London during October and November 1915. After these three issues the magazine ceased publication. Numbers 1-3 have never been bound in a volume.

gle family. In each episode some point is reached at which a principal character is made to realize that his awareness of the meaning and form of his experience is inadequate. Out of the "unknown," like God speaking to Abraham, comes the demand that he or she must *change*, must abandon his or her ordinary self, enter into a kind of death, and emerge reborn, transfigured through his submission to the fate which reaches him as an emanation from beyond the known world where he has been accustomed to find his *raison d'être*. All the principal characters receive this call to enter upon a transfigured relation to life. But their responses are various. Tom and Lydia Brangwen in the first generation submit and are saved; in the second generation Will and Anna Brangwen progress toward wholeness of being but fall short; in the last generation Ursula Brangwen, after a series of exhausting erotic experiences, is prepared for the final transfiguration, and only awaits "the man out of Eternity" with whom she can reach her goal, while her suitor at the end is moving away toward personal disintegration, his back turned on grace.

Why do some of these characters succeed in saving themselves while others fail? This question is virtually impossible to answer. Tom Brangwen is shown as a decent but ignorant man who possesses no exceptional gifts of spiritual or intellectual penetration, while his wife Lydia is first presented as a dispirited widow whom an earlier marriage had reduced to physical and nervous exhaustion. Yet this couple attains to "the perpetual wonder of the transfiguration." On the other hand, Will and Anna, who begin married life together with the advantages of youth, vitality, and an intense love for each other, become involved in an obscure battle of wills which continues year after year and is given up only when both characters see that their differences will never be resolved. No explanation of this uneven distribution of rewards is given anywhere in the novel. The failure of Will's and Anna's marriage cannot be traced to any clearly defined moral or psychological flaw in either character. We remember here that in his letter Lawrence disavowed a concern for consistency of character, so it will do no good to study and restudy the characters of Will and Anna. We must fall back upon the "inhuman will" then, but our difficulty here is that nothing can be said about this mystery. Its workings are as arbitrary as any power of grace which one might find operative in the works of a Christian author.

To illustrate this point, the following description of a flaw in Will's "essential" being may be cited:

> He was aware of some limit to himself, of something unformed in his very being, of some buds which were not ripe in him, some folded centres of darkness which would never develop and unfold whilst he was alive in the body. He was unready for fulfilment. Something undeveloped in him limited him, there was a darkness in him which he *could* not unfold, which would never unfold in him. (p. 207)

The narrator knows all, sees all, but can deliver himself of the truth only in shadowy similitudes. The reader cannot challenge this outcome, because he is never in a position to develop an understanding of "folded centres of darkness" on his own. If the character is gripped by the inhuman will of life, the reader is in the hands of a narrator who keeps secret some of the ultimate issues of life and death his characters face.

I do not mean to suggest that *The Rainbow* contains no scenes of the traditional kind where character is revealed through action, or that it lacks passages of acute psychological analysis where less "essential" levels of being are lucidly described. Such sections as the extended account of

Ursula's teaching experiences (Chapter XIII: "The Man's World") or the account given of the intense and unhealthy intimacy between the child Ursula and her slightly sadistic father are beautifully specified and rich in original insights into the complexities of social and psychological relationships. But when the narrator deals with essential being, when he describes ultimate shifts of awareness experienced by certain characters, their ordinary social and psychological selves are no longer relevant to his concerns. He abandons ordinary reality and attempts to win the reader's assent by suggesting that there exists another kind of essential reality in terms of which certain shifts of attitude and developments of the action which seem arbitrary are in fact revelations of a destiny.

The creation of this *other* reality was Lawrence's way of embodying his sense of the inhuman will and essential being in palpable form. Tonal and symbolic suggestiveness became the means by which Lawrence attempted to show the operation of these unknowable forces of life within the self and within society. Now it is time to examine these means to consider whether they adequately perform the tasks assigned to them.

If most readers find the narrative art of *The Rainbow* original, difficult, occasionally hallucinated and occasionally almost boring, their response depends mainly on Lawrence's experiments with narrative tone and on the recurrent use of three forms of symbolism: expanding symbols, symbolic characters, and symbolic ritual scenes. If one tries to imagine what the novel would have been like without these devices for the enlargement of meaning it seems clear that *The Rainbow* would have emerged as a kind of naturalistic slice-of-life, recording without tragic or humorous coloring typical experiences of a family over the course of three generations. Tom is a yeoman farmer tied to the land; his son-in-law is first a village craftsman and then an art teacher in a county seat; his granddaughter is trained at a university and comes to enjoy the friendship of artistic and upper-class people in London. These changes reflect three-quarters of a century of English social history. Such a subject naturalistically treated might have appealed to Arnold Bennett, but Lawrence, who wished to irradiate life's surface with a visionary light, to reveal an extraordinariness inherent in the ordinary, found it necessary to work in a new way with the domestic facts of average experience.

NARRATIVE TONE, RHYTHM, AND METAPHOR

Here are three short passages excerpted from different parts of the book.

1.

Their lives and interrelations were such; feeling the pulse and body of the soil, that opened to their furrow for the grain, and became smooth and supple after their ploughing, and clung to their feet with a weight that pulled like desire, lying hard and unresponsive when the crops were to be shorn away. The young corn waved and was silken, and the luster slid along the limbs of the men who saw it. They took the udder of the cows, the cows yielded milk and pulse against the hands of the men, the pulse of the blood of the teats of the cows beat into the pulse of the hands of the men. They mounted their horses, and held life between the grip of their knees, they harnessed their horses at the wagon, and, with hand on the bridle-rings, drew the heaving of the horses after their will.   (p. 2)

2.

He turned and looked for a chair, and keeping her still in his arms, sat down with her close to him, to his breast. Then, for a few seconds, he went utterly to sleep, asleep and sealed in the darkest sleep, utter, extreme oblivion.

From which he came to gradually, always holding her warm and close upon him, and she as utterly silent as he, involved in the same oblivion, the fecund darkness.

He returned gradually, but newly created, as after a gestation, a new birth, in the womb of darkness. Aerial and light everything was, new as a morning, fresh and newly-begun. Like a dawn the newness and the bliss filled in. And she sat utterly still with him, as if in the same.

Then she looked up at him, the wide, young eyes blazing with light. And he bent down and kissed her on the lips. And the dawn blazed in them, their new life came to pass, it was beyond all conceiving good, it was so good, that it was almost like a passing-away, a trespass.   (pp. 40-41)

3.

And ever and again, the pure love came in sunbeams between them, when she was like a flower in the sun to him, so beautiful, so shining, so intensely dear that he could scarcely bear it. Then as if his soul had six wings of bliss he stood absorbed in praise, feeling the radiance from the Almighty beat through him like a pulse, as he stood in the upright flame of praise, transmitting the pulse of Creation.

And ever and again he appeared to her as the dread flame of power. Sometimes, when he stood in the doorway, his face lit up, he seemed like an Annunciation to her, her heart beat fast. And she watched him, suspended. He had a dark, burning being that she dreaded and resisted. She was subject to him as to the Angel of the Presence. She waited upon him and heard his will, and she trembled in his service.

Then all this passed away.   (p. 167)

The first passage describes the condition of "blood-intimacy" with the hot life of organic creation enjoyed by early generations of Brangwens. The powerfully rhythmic phrasing of the description seems designed to re-create in language an equivalent of the condition itself. This prose does its work on the reader's nerves, compelling imaginative assent from below the threshold of consciousness. "They" remain shadowy figures, as much demi-gods as men, scarcely differentiated from the life in which they are involved. Lawrence is trying not so much to make a reader see men, grain, horses, cows, and so forth as to make him sense a particular condition of life. The narrator remains in complete charge, never restating the substance of the passage in dramatic as opposed to descriptive terms. In *The Rainbow* as a whole the ratio of descriptive passages to dramatic scenes remains staggeringly disproportionate.

The second excerpt records a moment in the courtship of Tom Brangwen and Lydia Lensky. Here the narrator attempts through incremental repetition, images of darkness and light, deliberately imprecise metaphors like "womb of darkness" and "new birth" to indicate a larger meaning in this emotional experience. No precision is possible because the larger meaning is somehow bound up with an indefinable shift of human consciousness into an obscure realm of awareness, a realm of sleep and shadow. The clause "their new life came to pass" and the succeeding play on words effectively transfers the power of will and action from the human actors to an invisible, transcendent agency. Tom and Lydia do not choose their new life. It chooses them. They are the unwitting objects of an unknowable power.

The third passage describes successive phases of affection and hostility in the marriage of Anna and Will Brangwen. The religious similes and metaphors do not make clear to the reader's eye the two figures described; and they certainly do not help to clarify the nature and cause of an incompatibility between wife and husband. Instead Anna and Will dissolve and vanish, to be replaced by the figure of a flower, the Blessed Virgin, and an angel who is three different archangels by turns. What is the dark yet burning condition of being in Will which Anna fears? We know that it is some condition well beyond the powers of a marriage counselor to alleviate, but we know little else. As in the second passage, the question of causality is referred in the last sentence to an invisible agency. These states of love and of tension, like the metaphorical conversions which express them, come and go "and ever and again." They do not yield to intellectual scrutiny, and the married pair are doomed to live out the pattern of ambivalence with very little control over the direction their experience takes.

These passages are typical of many in *The Rainbow* where the narrative uses the devices of incremental repetition, striking metaphor, and incantatory rhythm to cast a penumbra over everyday events. They show Lawrence's attempt to articulate the mystery of the inhuman self and the forces to which it responds in a language that can mediate between what is visibly going on and what is going on "essentially." The strain on language is considerable and the strain on the reader can be unconscionable when passages of this sort continue too long and are not played off against dramatic scenes.

EXPANDING SYMBOLS:
ARCH, RAINBOW, CATHEDRAL

The major expanding symbols of this novel—the figures of the arch, rainbow, and cathedral—compose an elaborate structure of meanings in themselves, and it will now be useful to consider the question of the relation of this structure to the design of *The Rainbow* as a whole. The arch figure is introduced early, during a description of an unhappy moment in the marriage of Tom and Lydia Brangwen. Lydia is pregnant and has "lapsed into a sort of som-

bre exclusion, a curious communion with mysterious powers, a sort of mystic, dark state." Tom is frightened and
depressed by her change of mood. His state of anxiety is
imaged in the simile of a broken arch:

> The tension in the room was overpowering, it was difficult
> for him to move his head. He sat with every nerve, every
> vein, every fibre of muscle in his body stretched on a tension.
> He felt like a broken arch thrust sickeningly out from sup-
> port. For her response was gone, he thrust at nothing. And
> he remained himself, he saved himself from crashing down
> into nothingness, from being squandered into fragments,
> by sheer tension, sheer backward resistance.   (p. 60)

In the course of over four hundred more pages of narrative this visual figure of the arch undergoes a remarkable development. Beginning here as a simple simile it
grows and changes into the dominant image of the rainbow,
central symbol of the book, symbol of a transfigured self
and a perfected marriage relation, and finally on the last
page the prophetic symbol of a promised transformation of
human life on earth:

> And the rainbow stood on the earth. She knew that the
> sordid people who crept hard-scaled and separate on the
> face of the world's corruption were living still, that the
> rainbow was arched in their blood and would quiver to life
> in their spirit, that they would cast off their horny covering
> of disintegration, that new, clean, naked bodies would issue
> to a new germination, to a new growth, rising to the light
> and the wind and the clean rain of heaven. She saw in the
> rainbow the earth's new architecture, the old, brittle cor-
> ruption of houses and factories swept away, the world built
> up in a living fabric of Truth, fitting to the over-arching
> heaven.   (p. 495)

Like this passage, the other two passages[5] in which the

[5] See *The Rainbow*, pp. 90-92, 192-193.

rainbow makes its appearance are marked by unusual beauty and power, considered in themselves. The figure is invoked once as a symbol of the wholeness of being achieved by Tom and Lydia through their marriage, and, once again, surprisingly, to conclude the main part of the episode in which the rather less wholesome marital experiences of Anna and Will are narrated. At the end of the novel it is Ursula, just recovering from a nervous breakdown and ensuing miscarriage of an unwanted child, to whom the climactic, transfiguring vision is vouchsafed. Clearly, the symbol cannot be consistently defined in dramatic terms. It does not always illuminate or become illuminated by the various turns of the plot or by what we come to know of the principal characters as the story moves along. Each time we encounter the symbol we must in effect forget where we have gotten to in the novel and move onto a sacred ground of quasi-religious contemplation.

What I am trying to get at here is that the visionary value implied by the rainbow figure is frequently incommensurate with the level of ordinary reality on which a majority of the narrated events take place. Lawrence posits a relation he cannot show. The symbol expresses a prophetic hope instead of the ultimate truth of the human condition the novel's episodes narrate. It is Lawrence rather than the neurotic Ursula who sees the rainbow arched in the blood and quivering to life in the spirit. Lawrence has difficulty fusing the social character and the "essential being" of his actors into one presentation. The reader remains doubtful that a Tom, a Lydia, an Anna Brangwen are worthy of the visionary accolade the rainbow figure confers. For *The Rainbow* to have been altogether successful, the surface of experience must have been so irradiated by a visionary light that a reader would have encountered the luminousness of essential being in the most commonplace gestures, attitudes, and encounters of the characters. Instead of this integration there is usually an oscillation between two distinct modes of being. In one mode Ursula is no better than she should be—certainly no better than her discarded lover—and Anna is a complacent, fruitful and thoroughly commonplace English mum. In another mode these same people are radiant expressions of the Life Force. As such they belong to the company of the rainbow, but only by an accident of nomenclature is the reader in a position to connect the two distinct selves inhabiting them.

As it happens, there is a dominant symbol in *The Rainbow* which *is* brilliantly integrated with an important dramatic sequence—the symbol of the cathedral. Unlike the rainbow, the cathedral is not only a concrete object, but a church building in the city of Lincoln as well. As symbol the cathedral stands in competitive relation with the rainbow. The rounded arch of the latter lifts into the heavens and returns to earth; that is, it symbolizes a form of self-realization wherein the values of blood and spirit, of organic unison with nature and a higher spiritual expression, are kept in a state of vibrant tension. Moreover, since marriage is the enterprise through which this form of fulfillment becomes possible, the rainbow is a symbol of marriage. The wedding of opposites in marriage leads not to a static condition of contentment but into a perpetual journey of self-discovery and discovery of the marriage partner. The emphasis is on becoming; the shifting, dissolving color patterns of a rainbow are appropriate to this emphasis. By contrast, the pointed stone arch of the Gothic cathedral symbolizes a mystic mergence with Godhead. It is a consummation in which the solitary human soul leaps free of earth to become absorbed into a spiritual realm:

> Here the stone leapt up from the plain of earth, leapt
> up in a manifold, clustered desire each time, up, away from

the horizontal earth, through twilight and dusk and the
whole range of desire, through the swerving, the declina-
tion, ah, to the ecstasy, the touch, to the meeting and the
consummation, the meeting, the clasp, the close embrace,
the neutrality, the perfect, swooning consummation, the
timeless ecstasy. There his soul remained, at the apex of the
arch, clinched in the timeless ecstasy, consummated. (p.199)

This is of course a description of Will Brangwen's experience, taken from Chapter VII: "The Cathedral."

In that chapter difficulties develop because of a sharp,
irreconcilable difference in the life attitudes of husband and
wife. Will is a dark, inchoate soul, interested in religious
art from a standpoint at once spiritual and aesthetic, indifferent to a public career in the outer world of society.
He is both pious and sensual. Anna, on the other hand, is
a cheerful rationalist who rejects religion as a lugubrious
collection of old wives' tales. Her interests are centered
in the home, in the endless and prosaic details of domesticity.

Early in the episode the couple's differences become
focused in a quarrel over religious symbols, specifically over
the meaning of the ecclesiastical symbol of *Agnus Dei* and
the question whether the miracle at Cana was genuine. This
quarrel is only one expression of a basic misunderstanding
between Will and Anna which interferes with their physical
relations as well as with their casual domestic associations
in the home. But Lawrence chooses to fix this difference
in terms of religious attitudes. He brings the issue to a
climax in Chapter VII. Here the couple visits Lincoln
Cathedral together, and while Will hurls himself aloft in
mystic communion Anna continues to go her own way along
the ground:

She was not to be flung forward on the lift and lift of
passionate flights, to be cast at last upon the altar steps as

57

upon the shore of the unknown. There was a great joy
and a verity in it. But even in the dazed swoon of the
cathedral, she claimed another right. The altar was barren,
its lights gone out. God burned no more in that bush. It was
dead matter lying there. She claimed the right to freedom
above her, higher than the roof.   (p. 200)

She forces Will to look at the carved gargoyle faces
whose winks and leers gave "suggestion of the many things
that had been left out of the great concept of the church."
Standing together under the high roof of the church, they
engage in a final struggle which is really a quarrel between
two opposed valuations of the human situation. Anna is
victorious. Will loses his faith in the absolute and the cathedral is reduced in his eyes to a "shapely heap of dead matter . . . dead, dead." There is something piteous in all this.
Will's defeat condenses into a few agonized moments the
historic decline of Christian faith during the past century
or so. It is especially sad because the narrator confers on
Will no alternative form of fulfillment. He is not to become one of the transfigured company of the rainbow. In
this struggle Lawrence is on the side of Anna. In a sense
it is *his* symbol against the church's, and the outcome is
foreordained.

Nevertheless, one does not feel in this sequence that the
human situation has been contrived merely to illustrate a
prophetic hope or a doctrine. The symbols serve the dramatic pattern at least as effectively as the dramatic situation permits Lawrence to confront and triumph over the
great institution of the church. The cathedral scene symbolically brings into play not only a controversy over values, but also an entire range of differences agitating a human relationship. Lawrence saw with unusual distinctness
that various aspects of behavior which are separated from
one another in superficial discussions about life really go

together. A religious attitude is actually an expression of the whole man. Will's sensuality and his mysticism are opposite sides of the same coin. In sex and in worship he sought to merge himself in an undifferentiated obscurity, while resisting the imperative of individuation. No complex enterprise such as marriage can survive on an exclusively instinctual basis, and Anna's resistance to his religious strivings, like her resistance to his regressive sexual instincts, combats Will's peculiar tendency to fight away from the light of the daytime world toward a state of absorbed inertia. Anna represents society as much as she represents Lawrence in this episode, and the problem of combining living selves with social forms so as to create a new kind of narrative art is for once successfully surmounted.

SYMBOLIC CHARACTERS

In the latter part of the novel, when the narrative focus is concentrated on Ursula Brangwen, Lawrence introduces a series of minor characters who act almost as signposts pointing directions which the questing heroine must become aware of if she is to attain in her own way to "the perpetual wonder of transfiguration." This symbolic device is not elaborated. None of these characters interacts with Ursula more than briefly, and as signs they all express an identical meaning.

The characters are the bargee whom Ursula encounters while out walking with Anton (pp. 309-314); Anthony Schofield, the brother of her friend Maggie (pp. 413-417); and, finally, the taxi driver who takes Ursula and Anton back to their hotel after she has told Anton she will never marry him (pp. 467-469). These three figures, and to some extent the situations in which they appear, recall the character of Annable in *The White Peacock* and his peculiar role. The bargeman's vessel is in fact named the Annabel and, like the gamekeeper's tumbledown cottage, has room for several healthy children, even though it is grimy with coal dust and cramped in its domestic arrangements. Anthony Schofield resembles Annable in the wood-demon aspect. He is faunlike and his eyes have the gleam of a satyr's; they are "the pale grey eyes of a goat." When this lover of life in the outdoors looks at Ursula, it is "as an animal might." Ursula encounters these two men in woodland settings, but the third man turns up in the midst of the city. All we get is a brief glimpse of him, a dark "animal face" whose flickering glance strikes fear into her.

The importance of the bargeman and the taxi driver depends on the immediate situations in which they appear. When Ursula meets the bargeman she has been arguing with Anton against a career in which the individual subordinates himself to and becomes an anonymous part of a great common enterprise of the State. It will be noted that this dispute roughly parallels the dispute about mystic mergence with the Divine that raged between Will and Anna. Ursula contemptuously rejects the ideal of impersonal service and tells Anton that for her he does not even seem to exist: "You seem like nothing to me." Immediately thereafter she notices the barge tied up at a canal lock beside the path where they have been walking and moves forward to meet the keeper and his family. We have encountered a very similar sequence in *The White Peacock*. There it was Lettie Beardsall who had been walking with her fiancé, Leslie Tempest, and had come upon a field of snow drops. After communing with the flowers she had looked up at her lover and remarked, "You do not seem real to me." And then Annable had loomed up suddenly, "like some malicious Pan."

In *The Rainbow* Anton has already been revealed as prepared to sacrifice his life for an abstraction called the State.

This sacrifice involves a suppression of individual instinct and emotion, and of all those habits of ordinary life which Lawrence is disposed to consider real. The bargeman, an ordinary mortal caring nothing for the great tasks of imperialism to which Anton wishes to dedicate himself through military service, a man involved in fatherhood, daily labor, simple recreations, is to Ursula the embodiment of what is most valuable in existence. He is oriented in physical experience, unhaunted by the conventions and abstractions of modern culture, satisfied to inhabit his own body. To us he represents perhaps no more than a simple truth, but to Lawrence this truth was the greatest of those forgotten by the unhappy people of our era. To Ursula he is a reminder that fulfillment lies elsewhere than in a life with Anton. She cannot go live on a barge—she is too well-educated, too intellectually self-aware for this pastoral reversion—but she must find a way of including in her future the value which the bargeman represents. When she gives her name and necklace to the bargeman's child, it is a kind of rite in which kinship is established between them. It is also a recognition that they are already akin.

The feral taxi driver is another symbolic foil to Anton, who is here depicted as suffering the fate which awaits all those who begin by worshipping abstractions and end by becoming abstractions themselves. Why should Anton shatter into fragments at Ursula's refusal to marry him? Because he has become hollow and has looked to Ursula to create in him that illusion of livingness without which he cannot face the world. A little earlier Ursula had cried, "I'm against you, and all your old, dead things." He had responded with these agonized reflections:

> She seemed, with the last words, uttered in hard knowl-
> edge, to strike down the flag that he kept flying. He felt
> cut off at the knees, a figure made worthless. A horrible

sickness gripped him, as if his legs were really cut away, and he could not move, but remained a crippled trunk, dependent, worthless. The ghastly sense of helplessness, as if he were a mere figure that did not exist vitally, made him mad, beside himself.   (pp. 461-462)

It is a short step from this to the figure of the crippled Sir Clifford Chatterley in Lawrence's last novel. Sir Clifford is a war hero, but this merely counts against him in Lawrence's view. His handicaps are the outward sign of an inner failure in "vital" existence, more to be censured than pitied. The first of these devitalized figures to appear in a full-length Lawrence novel was Leslie Tempest in *The White Peacock*. There the heroine had refused to marry him during his convalescence from a motor car accident—illness is constantly in the background when Lawrence treats this theme of abstraction *versus* the reality of physical experience —and he had behaved exactly as Anton does in the restaurant and during the taxicab ride. He had undergone a hysterical crisis of tears and hiccups, revealing to the uneasy reader his condition of disintegratedness.

Where is the taxi man in all this? I should say that he is an expression of sheer vitality, of the power of the physical element in experience, something that Anton, or for that matter, Leslie and Sir Clifford sacrifice in their careers as they cling to one kind of devitalizing conformism or another. Made manifest in the driver, this elemental value appears as a lowest common denominator, a brute fact, a Caliban. This animal-man has none of the kindliness of the bargekeeper, none of the grace of Anthony. From one standpoint, he is nothing more than the extruded core of physical being which an Anton no longer possesses. Nothing can disintegrate *him*, although again he can represent no simple solution to the problems which Ursula faces. According to the nature of the double imperative, the driver signifies no more than a half-truth; as he appears in this scene he is only the suggestion of a necessary truth which is more clearly revealed in the bargekeeper incident and finally forced on the reluctant girl when she is chased by visionary horses in the novel's extraordinary penultimate scene.

THE RITUAL SCENES

These scenes are "rituals" because they dramatize, frequently in solemn ceremonial gesture and in a ceremonious prose, the ultimate relation of the "essential" man or woman —usually it is a woman—to what Lawrence calls the "unknown." As such they are analogous with religious rites in which the relation of the human soul to God is celebrated. In these scenes "the old stable ego" of the character shatters, and the individual becomes unrecognizable in his everyday aspect. "Daytime consciousness" is suspended; the individual is described as coming under the direct influence of irresistible forces of life. Behavior under these circumstances may be assumed to express an ultimate of the human condition, the inhuman "isness" of the self. These scenes present an artistic proof that essential being exists and indicate its nature. In them the individual is created anew, in a set of terms distinct from the dramatic and descriptive language used to define the same character as a social being.

There are five of the scenes altogether: the extended description of Lydia's slow emergence from the state of quiescent withdrawal she had suffered after the death of her first husband (pp. 45-50); the dancelike gathering of the sheaves performed by Will and Anna on a moonlit night during their courtship (pp. 116-120); the scene in which Anna Brangwen, pregnant and naked, dances before the "Unknown" as David danced before the Lord (pp. 179-181); Ursula's "moon-consummation" in the stack-yard (pp. 316-320); Ursula's encounter with the horses (pp. 485-490). They are composed for the most part through the narrator's descriptions; there is little opportunity for the use of a dramatic method, since the characters are not primarily interacting with one another but with mute natural forces. Now I should like to examine three of these scenes in detail.

Lydia's "new parturition" does not result from any conscious aim to make a new attempt after happiness. She wants to rest, but the Life Force, working in the succession of the seasons and making itself manifest in flowers, bees, and thrushes' eggs, causes "her soul" to rouse itself to attention. She cannot help herself. Although she consciously prefers withdrawal from life, Nature reaches out for her and brings her up from her walk in "the Underworld, where the shades throng intelligibly but have no connection with one." Lawrence's images define the essential Lydia, who cannot break her organic bond with life even though she wishes to die, in terms of a perennial flower which withdraws under the surface of the earth into its seed and is reborn according to ineluctable biological necessity, under the beneficent influence of a warm spring. His metaphor of the Underworld merges Lydia with the figure of Persephone, who in the vegetation myth returns to the upper world after her sojourn in Hades. When the reader comes to view Lydia in these metaphorical terms, his understanding of her and her plight becomes transformed. The *gestalt* of her moral-psychological character becomes indistinct. As her outlines dissolve she flows into the greater life of organic nature.

These images of the flower and the seed are not sentimental metaphorical projections of a psychological condition. The suggestion is that the essence of Lydia and the essence of the flower are the same; and it is implied that if she is to flourish once again in the daytime world she must be returned temporarily to the organic, instinctual source of creation, there to be recharged with vitality. Lawrence had begun as early as his first novel to suggest through images and metaphors an intimate connection between the outer world of nature and the inner world of the individual. But it was still possible in *The White Peacock* for the reader to assume that the author was exploiting sentimentally the great Pathetic Fallacy of romanticism. Here we have passed beyond loose analogy to a position which identifies concretely the essence of the human with the essence of the natural. Lydia "inhumanly" and both Lydia and the flower "physiologically" respond to the mysterious Will of life, which replaces the Will of God as prime mover. Hulme's prophecy is exactly fulfilled.

The artistic strategy of the sheave-gathering scene involves the use of incremental repetition in combination with vivid imagery to suggest that Will and Anna enact in their sensual pursuit of and retreat from one another the larger rhythms of the "living cosmos." Will wishes to kiss Anna. This desire arises in ordinary consciousness. But in reaching after her he is seized upon by the Life Force. His ordinary will is replaced by "a low, deep-sounding will in him, which vibrated to her, tried to set her in accord, tried to bring her gradually to him, to a meeting, till they should be together, till they should meet as the sheaves that swished together." This inscrutable will becomes the agent, and the young man becomes the instrument of its massive urge toward "accord." As long as this will continues to vibrate, the dancelike approaches and retreats of the two lovers are controlled by a power outside themselves, a power whose operation blurs the distinction between the sexual impulses of two young lovers and the general dynamic relation which all parts of living nature hold to one another.

This scene in no way prepares us for the ensuing narration of the frequently unhappy, even sordid, marital relations of Will and Anna. There is little reason why this experience should have happened to them rather than to some other characters. In other words, whatever happy meaning we choose to read from this scene, it is not one that is continuously supported and amplified by later developments in the careers of the two characters. As husband and wife, mother and father, Will and Anna fail to live up to the inhuman selves they expose in this scene. As a design, the sheave-gathering scene remains a thing in itself; its actors are really symbols, and the meaning of the symbols has little to do with the actual couple who live out their marital career and raise seven children in the village of Cossethay and in the provincial town of Beldover.

Ursula's encounter with the horses cannot be criticized from exactly the same point of view. It seems a meaningful outcome of experiences she has already undergone as an ordinary human being. Ursula in *The Rainbow* is a sort of female Quixote who passes through one experience after another in quest of her "true self." Her activities cover a considerable range: an adolescent love affair, a Lesbian attachment, two years as pupil-teacher in a grade school, a broken engagement, three years as a university student. In each circumstance Ursula finds that the elusive goal of self-realization and the elusive definition of the true self are still beyond her. At last, when she has discovered that she is with child by her discarded lover, she comes to realize that she has been pursuing a will-of-the-wisp:

> What did the self, the form of life matter? Only the living from day to day mattered, the beloved existence in the body, rich, peaceful, complete, with no beyond, no further trouble, no further complication. (p. 483)

She then writes a letter to Skrebensky, humbly asking him to take her back, and when she has finished it she feels "that now, now she was at the depths of herself. This man was her true self forever. With this document she would appear before God at the Judgement Day."

Perhaps for many novelists such a point of moral awareness would be sufficient, but the two-phased Laurentian moral imperative is directly opposed to this attempt at compromise. As Ursula goes walking in the woods after writing the letter she becomes dimly conscious of "a gathering restiveness, a tumult impending within her." This tumult we must take as the voice of her submerged "essential" nature signaling her that she must continue her search after wholeness. As the scene continues the inner turbulence is projected outside Ursula and becomes embodied in the herd of horses which races up and down before her until, on the verge of physical and nervous collapse, she manages to escape from the field where she has encountered them. Her escape is in some sense an exit from the wilderness of instinctive experience, back to the "ordered world of men." Whether these horses are a hallucination or really there, they symbolize the power of the life of instinct, the life which underlies the upper layers of the self, underlies the accretions of moral and psychological conditioning that hide the deep, turbulent impulses of "flesh" and "blood" in every individual. Ursula is harried by her own interior horses, grotesque as that may sound, but we must assume that the image of the trampling herd is a valid symbol for the deep instinctive life of all of us.

> She was aware of their breasts gripped, clenched narrow in a hold that never relaxed, she was aware of their red nostrils flaming with long endurance, and of their haunches, so rounded, so massive, pressing, pressing, pressing to burst the grip upon their breasts, pressing for ever till they went mad, running against the walls of time, and never bursting free. (p. 487)

These anarchic, archetypal horses must be confined, but they and their pressure are real enough. Ursula's compromise is a denial of the life inside her. She is punished by suffering this visionary confrontation and simultaneously she is "saved" by being brought face to face with a truth about herself and about life, the denial of which could only lead to a kind of death-in-life. For it is clear that although these horses are profoundly dangerous to "the ordered world," the power they symbolize is to be taken as the ultimate energic source of man's vitality, his creativity, and of whatever is vital in civilized society as well.

This compelling scene is disappointing only in the aftermath. Ursula's experience was designed to illuminate for her the paths of error into which she had wandered in the conduct of her life. Deeply corrupted by her experience in the daytime world, she had lost touch with vital instinct and now the structure of her character must be broken down. She must be reduced to a surd of elemental being, later to be reconstituted as a wholesome human individual:

> As she sat there, spent, time and the flux of change passed away from her, she lay as if unconscious upon the bed of the stream, like a stone, unconscious, unchanging, unchangeable, whilst everything rolled by in transience, leaving her there, a stone at rest on the bed of the stream, inalterable and passive, sunk to the bottom of all change. (p. 489)

The reader awaits impatiently the account of some new growth which must come to this person who has adventured so much and suffered so much in the past. But Lawrence cannot, or at least does not, even begin to indicate the mode of this new growth. We are told that Ursula now possesses "a deep, inalterable knowledge." We view the first stirrings of her renewal in the familiar metaphor of a "naked, clear kernel thrusting forth the clear, powerful shoot," and we hear that Ursula has reached the shore of the unknown land "after crossing the void." Finally, we are given the vision of the rainbow arching over the world's corruption, and the novel sings itself out with no definition of the new Ursula, or description of the unknown land she has entered.

The Rainbow is in a sense Lawrence's sacred book. It is therefore not surprising that he should have adapted material from religious tradition[6] to his secular but visionary ends, especially since Lawrence saw religious myths as "images of human experience." The succession of familial generations which the novel describes, its theme of continuity through change, its embodiment of the notion that in ordinary, everyday experience the individual is called to work out his salvation—all these features establish a significant parallel between the Brangwens ("a curious family, a law to themselves, separate from the world, isolated, a small republic set in invisible bounds") and one of those ancient biblical families like the clan of Noah or Abraham which carried God's promise in its table of genealogy. When the young Ursula dreams of that giant race before the flood, of the Sons of God who came in "unto the daughters of men and they bore children unto them," the image of these Old Testament titans is apt to blend in a reader's imagination with the former generations of Brangwen men who "lived full and surcharged, their senses full fed, their faces always turned to the heat of the blood, staring into

[6] The rainbow metaphor is borrowed from Genesis, where it is a sign of the new covenant between God and Noah. Tom Brangwen, patriarch of the family, is symbolically associated with Noah. In Chapter II his drunken speech on marriage at the meal following Anna's wedding corresponds to the biblical episode in which the drunken Noah is exposed before his sons. The biblical flood is reproduced in transposed position as the flash flood which bursts over the Marsh farm and drowns Tom. See IV: "The Marsh and the Flood."

the sun, dazed with looking toward the source of generation."

Certainly the pulsing, incantatory prose rhythms of *The
Rainbow* constantly recall the King James Version. Even
the narrative quality of the novel shares some characteristics
with the Bible stories. According to Erich Auerbach,[7] "in
the Old Testament stories, the sublime, tragic, and prob-
lematic take shape precisely in the domestic and commonplace"; "the peace of daily life in the house, in the fields,
in the flocks, is undermined by . . . the promise of a bless-
ing"; "the two realms of the sublime and everyday are
not only unseparated but basically unseparable." In his
general summary of biblical style Auerbach goes on to men-
tion "certain parts brought into high relief, others left
obscure, abruptness, suggestive influence of the unexpressed,
'background' quality." This last refers to what Auerbach
calls the "multilayeredness" of the characters in Old Testament narrative. It results from the fact that they are involved simultaneously with daily life and in a developing
relation to God the issue of which is salvation or perdition.

Up to a point these descriptions may be extended to *The
Rainbow*, for in this novel a fictional world is created in
which the possibility of transfiguration is always present in
the round of daily life; where multilayered characters like
Tom, Lydia, or Ursula stand ready to respond to the call
from the Unknown with the poignant affirmation of a
"Here am I." But there are difficulties, as soon as we remind ourselves that *The Rainbow* is, after all, a secular
book, and that Lawrence's inscrutable will of life is not the
same as the mysterious Divine Will of the Judaeo-Christian
tradition. I said earlier that Lawrence's concern with a real

[7] See *Mimesis: The Representation of Reality in Western Literature*,
trans. Willard Trask (Princeton: Princeton University Press, 1953),
pp. 12-13, 22-23.

livingness within the person was a concern for the freedom and integrity of people. While *The Rainbow* immensely deepens one's sense of vital human realities as they exist within history and society, and of vital forces of nature underlying civilization, it sometimes accomplishes this at the expense of Lawrence's original concern with freedom.

On a cynical view, it might be argued that Lawrence has invented a group of ordinary people, removed from them the power of moral choice and described them as being pushed toward an unknowable goal of self-realization by influences over which they have no control. While the characters sometimes obey imperatives recognizably moral, their obedience is often dictated to them from outside themselves. As we have seen, it is often difficult to compose into a single image Lawrence's vision of a transformed life and the "actual" lives of the characters. Beginning with the intention of revealing essential truth about the self Lawrence succeeds only in dissociating his characters into two incompatible levels of being.

On a view more adequate to the generous spirit of Lawrence's fundamental intention, it is certainly true that Lawrence did not fully succeed at the enormously difficult task of clarifying the relation of his "inhuman selves" to social roles on the one hand and to vital forces on the other. The difficulty was partly technical; after all, Lawrence had to invent numerous new aesthetic forms in order to reveal new aspects of reality and the drama of essential being. In the process he sometimes lost sight of the fact that salvation may seem a meaningless outcome unless consciously and vigorously sought. The outlook of the modern reader who sides with Anna against the Cathedral is still colored, or ought to be, by the ethical strenuousness of Christianity, which rings out in such pronouncements as "Seek and ye shall find!" We hesitate to judge Will Brangwen severely when we know so little of his "folded centres of darkness," to admire Ursula when the coming to pass of her new life, as described at the end, so closely resembles a state of deep neurotic depression. Nevertheless, except for this single clouded issue *The Rainbow* is one of the great advances in the art of the twentieth-century novel, conquering as it does vast new territories in the realm of human reality and creating new images of human destiny.

Women in Love, "a sequel to *The Rainbow* though quite unlike it,"[8] is Lawrence's most fully achieved book, his most difficult, and is one of the half dozen most important novels of the present century. When he had almost completed the final revision in November 1916, Lawrence wrote, "the book frightens me; it is so end-of-the-world," and we know he intended at one point to entitle the novel *Dies Irae*.[9] His description fits the thing done in at least three senses. Like *The Magic Mountain*, *Women in Love* sums up a society which did not survive the first world war and the convulsive revolutionary aftermath of the war. Secondly, it envisions prewar England—and Europe—as though it were already in its death throes. This process of dissolution is represented as going on in society at large, in the sphere of personal relations, in the hearts and souls of individual characters.

Gerald's obsessive tie to Gudrun leads to his own death, but Gerald's efficient reorganization of the Crich family

---

[8] Quoted by Richard Aldington in his introduction to the Phoenix edition of *Women in Love* (London: Heinemann, 1954), p. vii.

[9] *Letters*, p. 380.

mines has already spelled a kind of death for thousands of workmen by converting them into machine-men. As early as the ninth chapter we hear that Gudrun is "like a new Daphne, turning not into a tree but a machine." At the end, as she prepares to go off with the sculptor Loerke to enjoy a "frictional" relation of witty sensationalism, we understand that the metamorphosis is completed. Since the novel equates the machine principle with death, Gudrun has to be written off for good. Alive with Loerke, who is a kind of vampire figure like Hermione, she is deader than the frozen snowman she has deserted; for even in his dying Gerald retained some vestige of a human quality, if it was only his hysteria.

This process of dissolution is universal in the novel. It is the very form of the society represented and determines the nature of the human experience that can take place within the society. Rupert Birkin recognizes that it is going on in himself and coaxes Ursula toward the same self-recognition. He has been more deeply corrupted than she, through his love affair with Hermione, and is therefore more pessimistic than she about the possibilities of escape. Because he "bases his standard of values on pure being"— unlike Gerald, for whom the given societal forms represent ultimate standards—he does not mistake death for life. But he also assumes early on that his generation is involved in a *natural* cycle of destruction preceding a fresh cycle of creation into which neither he nor anyone else can survive:

"Oh yes, ultimately," he said. "It means a new cycle of creation after—but not for us. If it is the end, then we are the end—fleurs du mal, if you like. If we are fleurs du mal, we are not roses of happiness, and there you are."

"But I think I am," said Ursula. "I think I am a rose of happiness."

"Ready-made?" he asked ironically.

"No—real," she said, hurt.

"If we are the end, we are not the beginning," he said.

"Yes, we are," she said. "The beginning comes out of the end."

"After it, not out of it. After us, not out of us."

"You are a devil, you know, really," she said. "You want to destroy our hope. You *want* us to be deathly."

"No," he said. "I only want us to *know* what we are."

"Ha!" she cried in anger. "You only want us to know death."   (p. 165)

Ursula's task is to persuade Birkin to abandon his fatalism so that together they may begin to build life anew. Birkin's task is to make Ursula see that the world as she knows it, and the ideals of that world, are doomed. This means he must teach her to give up her conventional attitude toward love, because insofar as it *is* conventional, that is, conditioned by the present form of society, it is destructive. Also, he must prepare her for eventual flight from the known world. The task is difficult because their departure must literally be a journey into "nowhere," since "everywhere" the cycle of destruction grinds on. Ursula's task is difficult too. Birkin, who is deeply injured "in his soul" as the novel opens, and is almost slain by the frenzied Hermione soon after, is in no optimistic mood. But somehow the couple quarrel each other into a relationship which by the novel's end seems stronger than death.

A third sense in which *Women in Love* is "end-of-the world" is personal to Lawrence. For Lawrence, as for a great many other European artists of the period, the war came as the greatest shock of his entire life. He loathed the war, utterly disbelieved in the necessity of it, and tended to blame its outbreak on the perverse will of mankind in general. He keeps war out of the book, but cannot keep out the feeling the war had inspired in him. The vision of society-as-death reflects the cycle of destruction through which Europe was passing between 1914 and 1918. Lawrence's revulsion from his fellow man in wartime comes through in Birkin's gloating fantasies of the beauty of a world from which all traces of *homo sapiens* have been eliminated, and in Loerke's nihilistic fantasies of a superbomb that could split the world in two.

Despite these evidences of rage *Women in Love* is not misanthropic *au fond*. Lawrence treats Gerald with tenderness and compassion and all his characters with a characteristic detachment which people who do not know how to read Lawrence invariably take for violent prejudice. Loerke is loathsome, but he is also brave and gifted, just as Gudrun, though perverse, is vivid, beautiful, and self-sufficient. Birkin, who expresses some of Lawrence's cherished ideas, is often ridiculed for his self-consciousness and pedantry; some of the most amusing and happily written scenes are those in which Ursula argues him and his theories into the ground.

Nevertheless, the book demands a toughness and courage from the reader for which it is difficult to think of a parallel. When Birkin and Ursula agree to marry, one of the first things they do is send in written resignations from their jobs. Since Birkin is a school inspector and Ursula a teacher, we must accept the fact that the two liveliest people in a society of the dead and dying abandon the defenseless young to a fate which is destruction. They desert their posts and go off to make a separate peace, like Frederick Henry and Catherine Barclay of *A Farewell to Arms*. Yet that is just the point. Self-sacrifice and devotion to duty are anything but virtues, given the picture of the world Lawrence has created. After all, the zombielike Hermione yearns to sacrifice herself to Birkin, and one of the first things he tries to teach Ursula is that living selves are *not* to be sacrificed in love, war, work, or whatever. Gerald does his duty as he sees it. In obeying this essential imperative of a ruling class he freezes his own self to death and maims the selves of those who work for him.

Women in Love stands in somewhat the same relation to the real prewar world of England and Europe as one class of Science Fiction novel or Utopian novel stands in relation to actuality. Lawrence detects certain destructive tendencies in his society. He isolates and magnifies these tendencies, predicts their outcome, then merges an essentially apocalyptic vision with the particular segment of historical time he has in hand. The novel compresses reality instead of distorting it. The tone of the opening chapter, describing an upper-class church wedding, is purely Edwardian if not high Victorian. The final chapters, representing in terms of symbolic drama a condition of frozen entropy to which our society has not yet risen, is a prediction of where we may well end up rather than a description of where we were in 1910.

Women in Love is full, perhaps too full, of talk about ideas; but two ideas in particular, one an idea of fate, the other an idea of the fundamental nature of modern Western civilization, emerge as central determining assumptions from which most of the developments of the action stem. The first is adumbrated by Birkin in the second chapter when he is thinking over Gerald's accidental killing of his brother in early childhood.

> What then? Why seek to draw a brand and a curse across the life that had caused the accident? A man can live by accident, and die by accident. Or can he not? Is every man's life subject to pure accident, is it only the race, the genus, the species, that has a universal reference? Or is this not true, is there no such thing as pure accident? Has *every-thing* that happens a universal significance? Has it? Birkin,

pondering as he stood there, had forgotten Mrs. Crich, as she had forgotten him.

He did not believe that there was any such thing as accident. It all hung together, in the deepest sense. (p. 20)

Here Birkin gropes his way to the radical insight that everything that happens in a human career, including chance occurrences, is a revelation of the underlying qualities of being of the man or woman involved. It seems a desperately hard doctrine and not readily defensible. Yet in this particular case Ursula comes to a similar conclusion when in a conversation with Gudrun about the killing she remarks, "I wouldn't pull the trigger of the emptiest gun in the world, not if someone were looking down the barrel. One instinctively doesn't do it."

Ursula's version is easier to accept at once than Birkin's, because she suggests a reason why the accident is not an accident. If one instinctively doesn't do it, then there is some flaw in Gerald's instinctive equipment that enabled him to do it. In fact, Gerald suffers from a defect of "being" which is deadly, and he spreads his deadliness to Gudrun and to his workmen before he is finally disintegrated. Society as it is takes no account of being; it therefore offers Gerald power rather than a cure. Birkin, after diagnosing Gerald's disease, would like to cure him—his absurd proposal of *bludbruderschaft* and his jiu-jitsu wrestling match with him are efforts in that direction—but in the end he has to flee from the society of which Gerald is the finest flower and master as though from a plague.

How is it that society can accommodate itself to Gerald's defect, in fact reward him for it, but not to more wholesome beings like Ursula Brangwen and Rupert Birkin? In *The Rainbow* some dialogue was still possible between living selves and societal forms, at least in the pastoral generation to which Tom and Lydia belonged. Why has it ended? The

THE DEED OF LIFE

answer lies in the nature of the industrial system, which reaches a final perfection of form under Gerald's management. The following passage, describing the human consequences of the triumph of the machine principle in the Crich family mines, presents Lawrence's full case against the industrial system and against modern society:

> There was a new world, a new order, strict, terrible, inhuman, but satisfying in its very destructiveness. The men were satisfied to belong to the great and wonderful machine, even whilst it destroyed them. It was what they wanted. It was the highest that man had produced, the most wonderful and superhuman. They were exalted by belonging to this great and superhuman system which was beyond feeling or reason, something really godlike. Their hearts died within them, but their souls were satisfied. It was what they wanted. Otherwise Gerald could never have done what he did. He was just ahead of them in giving them what they wanted, this participation in a great and perfect system that subjected life to pure mathematical principles. This was a sort of freedom, the sort they really wanted. It was the first great step in undoing, the first great phase of chaos, the substitution of the mechanical principle for the organic, the destruction of the organic purpose, the organic unity, and the subordination of every organic unit to the great mechanical purpose. It was pure organic disintegration and pure mechanical organization. This is the first and finest state of chaos.   (p. 223)

The case is familiar enough and had been made before at least as early as Ruskin. Lawrence's paradox—that the perfection of a mechanical form is chaos—makes perfectly good sense in the light of his concern for the vitality of individual human beings which is destroyed when they subordinate themselves fully to pure mathematical principles of production and distribution. In "The Crown," Lawrence had defined wholeness of being as a conflict.

Eliminate the conflict and there is a collapse into chaos. Here the conflict has been resolved into system and order, and it is a chaos from the human standpoint. On the Laurentian view the perfect solution of a given human problem is in fact a dissolution, because it imposes rigid inorganic form on life, and the essence of life is change, variability, pulsation. "The wavering, indistinct, lambent" Birkin is alive by virtue of his "odd mobility and changeableness." His sudden shifts of attitude and feeling, his lapses of taste and logic, protect the life within him. Gerald, who is the soul of good social form, whose ideas are built up logically into lucid formulations, is wholly consistent on his white, gleaming surface but a chaos inside where his feelings are.

The industrial system, like the system of the medieval church to which Will Brangwen had been attracted, solves the problem of living in one mode only. It satisfies the economic needs of men and their hunger for order by arranging their activities according to an intellectualized, simplistic model of human reality. The workmen are satisfied in their souls but their hearts "died within them." The centers of their feeling dry up. They become walking dead like their masters, like the leisured classes which live off the profits of the system (Hermione), like the liberal intellectuals who opt for the social equality of man but accept the system itself (Sir Joshua Malleson), like the bohemians and courtesans infesting the fringes of this humanly decadent society, producing spectacular variants on the universal theme of dissolution (the habitués of the Café Pompadour), like the artists who serve the system by producing art according to the principle that "machinery and the acts of labor are extremely, maddeningly beautiful" (Loerke). In the deepest sense all things hang together, and all classes and groupings of a society whose mystique of production subordinates the organic to the mechanical share the same fate.

Lawrence is careful to avoid giving the impression that the decline of this society could be avoided through a reversion to mindlessness. The point of introducing the Pacific carving of the woman in labor and the West African statue of the Negro woman with the elongated neck is to show cultures which declined in a manner parallel to the decline of modern, white industrial society by fulfilling themselves in one mode at the expense of the wholeness of being which constitutes salvation for both selves and societies:

> It must have been thousands of years since her race had died, mystically: that is, since the relation between the senses and the outspoken mind had broken, leaving the experience all in one sort, mystically sensual. Thousands of years ago . . . the goodness, the holiness, the desire for creation and productive happiness must have lapsed, leaving the single impulse for knowledge in one sort, mindless progressive knowledge through the senses, knowledge arrested and ending in the senses, mystic knowledge in disintegration and dissolution. (pp. 245-246)

The point of arrest of Western industrial society is the same, only in the opposite mode. The same relation between mind and feeling has broken; desire for feeling has lapsed, leaving the single impulse to production, disembodied progressive industrial know-how, knowledge arrested in system-making. It is, equally, a knowledge in disintegration and dissolution.

So far *Women in Love* may sound like the sort of fictionalized essay or mere novel of ideas that a Charles Kingsley or an Aldous Huxley might have written. But Lawrence fully translates his criticisms of the character of a civilization into terms of human relationship and human drama. Gerald is the symbol of a social order and Birkin is the prophet of that order's doom; yet both men realize their destinies through personal relationships with women. The two relations, Gerald-Gudrun and Birkin-Ursula, intertwine throughout the book but represent wholly opposed experiences. If the latter is a drama of becoming, the former dramatizes coming apart. Becoming, by definition, has no final conclusion, so that the world of feeling into which Birkin and Ursula move remains as obscure as their ultimate destination after they have left England. Gerald's and Gudrun's drama of disintegration is, by contrast, horrifyingly lucid and moves to a frozen finality. Neither relation is a love affair in the usual sense of the word. Birkin refuses to admit that he wants love—although he comes at last to use that word about himself and Ursula—and Gerald confesses to Gudrun shortly before his death that he cannot love.

Like the other pair, Birkin and Ursula are attracted to each other at first sight. Ursula, just emerging from the state of numbed withdrawal she had endured in the closing pages of *The Rainbow*, swiftly recognizes that Birkin is a man she can love if he will once allow himself to come into focus, and he, as swiftly, realizes that she is the woman with whom he wants to flee the known world and its disease. Setting aside purely novelistic exigencies, their marriage is delayed only because Birkin, who appears to be as deeply injured by his experiences with people when the novel opens as Paul Morel had been at the end of *Sons and Lovers*, needs time to recover health, to work out an adequate theory of relationship, and to train Ursula in the principles of "star-equilibrium" which will determine the relation. There are elements of comedy implicit in this situation of which Lawrence is perfectly well aware, but the problems both people face are serious enough.

At first Ursula wants ordinary romantic love. She assumes that a marriage based on mutual self-sacrifice and mutual absorption, with plenty of sex thrown in, is the proper thing. Birkin, after his disastrous affair with Hermione, knows better. Hermione's will to serve him had proved a will to absorb him, a sort of hideous spiritual cannibalism. When he set his will against hers she had tried to kill him. He has learned the hard way that a will to do loving service can conceal a will to dominate, and treads warily before he involves himself again. If, in the famous chapter called "Moony" (XIX), when he stones the reflected image of the moon on the water, he is trying to break up the image of woman as triple goddess, as some critics have thought, then his action is the height of good sense. The three relations of *Magna Mater* to man are the mother who bears him, the mistress to whom he makes love, and mother earth who takes him inside her upon death. It is sheer folly for a grown man to seek to realize all three relations in one actual woman; since the first relation is entirely regressive, and the third deadly. Hermione, we must assume, had played the first two roles in Birkin's life for a time and aspired as well to the role of goddess of death, when he tried to end their affair.

In the same chapter Birkin suddenly stumbles upon the relation he wants, and it is anything but eccentric. In fact it is classic and normative as a definition of proper marriage.

> There was another way, the way of freedom. There was
> the paradisal entry into pure, single being, the individual
> soul taking precedence over love and desire for union,
> stronger than any pangs of emotion, a lovely state of free
> proud singleness, which accepted the obligation of the per-
> manent connection with others, and with the other, submits
> to the yoke and leash of love, but never forfeits its own

proud individual singleness, even while it loves and yields.
(p. 247)

Put as simply as possible, this idea of the association of man and woman insists that a decent self-respect must balance love and loyalty to the other. It stresses the permanency of the relationship, and concludes that each person must stand on his own feet, regardless of the regressive temptation to let the other person carry him or her throughout life. And by holding the idea of separateness in balance with the idea of union it exactly fulfills the marital ideal already described in *The Rainbow* as well as the requirement for wholeness of being that Lawrence has laid down.

When this idea is finally put to her clearly Ursula cannot help accepting it as a good one. Thus, there is little tension in their love affair of the Tristan and Isolde, Antony and Cleopatra love-death sort. But there are tension and poignancy in the utter contrast this sensible solution makes with the mad world of passion Gerald and Gudrun occupy, and with the civilized world as well. When Birkin and Ursula leave the snow valley they have nothing but their love as a career and a dwelling place. They must, somehow, generate a new world from their nucleus of relatedness, out of the intactness of the single being each possesses. Lawrence is always very moving when he represents his successful lovers flying in the face of civilized society, like Lot's family across the plains from Sodom. In *Women in Love* the account of the train journey from London, across Belgium toward the alpine resort where the Birkins will linger briefly with Gerald and Gudrun, powerfully conveys the pathos of departure toward an unknown future. Ursula remembers her childhood at the Marsh farm and reflects that "in one lifetime one travelled aeons." She sees the man sitting beside her as an utter stranger, but keeps her courage up. Just behind her lie a nasty scene with her father—the hapless Will Brangwen had responded to the news that she wanted to marry Birkin by striking her—and a hurried registry wedding. She and her husband are cut off from everything except each other and the sources of their own beings. But they are in love and therefore possess, as Birkin once put it, "the freedom together" that wholesome love is.

Gerald Crich, the agonist of *Women in Love*, stands under a kind of triple fatality from the beginning. He is the scion of a family whose vitality is mysteriously defective, who are "curiously bad at living," who "can do things but . . . cannot get on with life at all." Furthermore his nature has been adversely conditioned by the remarkable relation of "mutual interdestructivity" his parents have lived through, which has driven the mother into mental alienation and the father into cancer. Finally, he has his own particular defect, the instinctual flaw that enabled him to play Cain to his brother's Abel. Gerald may also be viewed as a kind of monstrous exaggeration of a characteristic late nineteenth-century English upper-class type, of the man who makes a brilliant administrative career by keeping his feelings under a control so severe that the feelings either turn nasty or die altogether. It is said of Gerald's father that even in the intolerable pain of his final illness he will not face what he actually feels about his wife, his career, about his own death. The same split between a mind which plans and commands and wills and the inner-feeling man is evident in Gerald, making him ideally suited to design a system of production in which living men and women become functions within a mathematical model. Under rigorous suppression Gerald's instinctive responses, already defective by inheritance, conditioning, and fate, turn chaotic. As the essential self begins to disintegrate, the feelings it originates turn destructive and self-destructive. Gerald cannot face the prospect of his own father's death without hysteria because he carries so much death inside him.

He moves in an atmosphere of "essential" death and decay. His early love affair is with the London courtesan Minette, to whom he is attracted by the film of disintegration in her eyes. Water is one of the principal symbols of dissolution in *Women in Love*, and Gerald is intimately associated with that symbol, first as a swimmer (Chapter IV: "Diver"); then in the scene where Gudrun is sketching water plants and he starts up before her "out of the mud," his hand like the stem of one of those plants growing in decay (Chapter X: "Sketchbook"); finally, as the organizer of the water party (Chapter XIV) which ends in the drowning of his sister and a young doctor. Gerald's fate is settled in that chapter. The cries of the drowning awaken him just as he is on the brink of an experience that might have begun his progress out of his condition of deathliness:

> His mind was almost submerged . . . into the things about him. For he always kept such a keen attentiveness, concentrated and unyielding in himself. Now he had let go, imperceptibly he was melting into oneness with the whole. It was like pure, perfect sleep, his first great sleep of life. He had been so insistent, so guarded, all his life. But here was sleep, and peace, and perfect lapsing out.   (p. 170)

After diving bravely into the dark waters until exhausted, he is brought ashore and says to Gudrun, "If you once die, then when it's over, it's finished. . . . There's room under that water there for thousands." He has seen his own death and is confirmed in the love of death. His life has some months to run, but he is effectively, vitally, finished.

As Birkin shrewdly observes of him early in the novel, Gerald is a potential victim looking to get his throat cut. If Birkin trains Ursula in the career of "star-equilibrium,"

Gerald trains Gudrun to be his tormenter and slayer. This is not evident at first. When Gudrun watches Gerald hold the terrified mare by means of whip and spur at the gate crossing while the engine passes, her identification with the mare suggests that she will play masochist to his sadist in the ensuing affair. But as time passes the pattern shifts. In the chapter called "Rabbit" (XVIII) they are approximately even, each gloating over the other's wounds. Yet she already harbors in her soul "an unconquerable desire for deep violence against him" and has actually struck him in the face after dancing the highland cattle to madness during the fête at Shortlands. When Gerald comes to her bedroom in Beldover he leaves a trail of clay linking up the grave of his father with the bed of his mistress. It is Gerald's trail, not Gudrun's. By permitting the affair to become the means of Gerald's death she is merely responding to Gerald's deepest will.

The scenes in the snow valley constitute the most brilliant writing that Lawrence ever did, and some of the finest writing in the history of the English novel as well. The valley is a real place and simultaneously a symbol of fate for both Gerald Crich and civilized society. Throughout the novel, his fairness and whiteness have been repeatedly emphasized and associated with the inhuman purity of his social ideas. Here where his vitality is at last to be bled white and empty by Gudrun's hatred, the mathematically perfect forms of snow flakes, composing a chaos of white, mock him and his concepts of fulfillment. It is a world all in one mode, a world without conflict or relief. Gerald as skier, as "snow-demon" is perfectly adapted to it and finally fuses with it when his being comes crashing down "in sheer nothingness" after Gudrun removes the last prop.

By a wonderful shift of emphasis, Lawrence wins for Gerald at the end our deepest sympathies. This is partly achieved through the sheer beauty of the descriptions of him in his isolation, as in the account of his climb upward after he has assaulted Loerke and Gudrun, or in the following paragraph from a few pages before that scene:

> So he came down reluctantly, snow-burned, snow-estranged, to the house in the hollow, between the knuckles of the mountain-tops. He saw its lights shining yellow, and he held back, wishing he need not go in to confront those people, to hear the turmoil of voices and to feel the confusion of other presences. He was isolated as if there were a vacuum round his heart, or a sheath of pure ice.   (p. 452)

But it is also partly done through the force of contrast between such descriptions and the accounts given of the revolting intimacies newly established between Loerke and Gudrun:

> Their whole correspondence was in a strange, barely comprehensible suggestivity, they kindled themselves at the subtle lust of the Egyptians or the Mexicans. The whole game was one of subtle inter-suggestivity, and they wanted to keep it on the plane of suggestion. From their verbal and physical nuances they got the highest satisfaction in the nerves, from a queer interchange of half-suggested ideas, looks, expressions, gestures.   (p. 439)

As is said, it is all suggestivity, and the suggestion here is that we are looking at a couple of robotic insects with exposed ganglia of fine wire consciously parodying human communication.

Given the choice the reader dies imaginatively with Gerald rather than make a threesome with the above creatures. Although Gudrun sees him finally as a boringly complex piece of machinery we see him as a man in the extremity and loneliness of his suffering. When Birkin sits grieving over Gerald's frozen body he wonders whether he had perished in the attempt to climb beyond the snows. If he had reached the crest he might have been able to descend into warm fertile valleys to the south. But then Birkin reflects, "Was it a way out. It was only a way in again." There is no escape. The snow of abstraction lies everywhere in the civilized world. Once a man or a society loses touch with its own deepest sources of being there is no way back. On the last page, Birkin permits himself the sentimental luxury of imagining that he could have saved Gerald by loving him in a union as eternal as his union with Ursula. But she is there at his elbow, thank God, to remind him with characteristic, Friedalike forthrightness that "you can't have it, because it's false, impossible." On that authoritative note they resume their journey into nowhere.

Women in Love is Lawrence's most perfectly integrated study of disintegration. His living selves are fully involved with a milieu thickly rendered and chillingly contemporary. If Lawrence's enterprise after *Sons and Lovers* had been to submit to the anguish of combining the living self with the shell of historical and social actuality his submission in his fifth novel has been complete. Unlike the dimly projected pastoral generations of the earlier Brangwens, who "held life between the grip of their knees," the heroes and heroines of *Women in Love* live close to the sick heart of a doomed civilization and are implicated in its final illness. The principal statement the novel makes is a deeply pessimistic one. It says that a living man or woman who embraces the social destiny offered by industrial Western society in the early twentieth century embraces his own dying. The anguish of combining has become a death anguish.

By contrast, *The Rainbow* is a very hopeful book. In that novel Lawrence could still believe that "the sordid people who crept hard-scaled and separate on the face of the world's corruption were living still," and "would issue to a new germination." This faith rested in turn on a deeper faith in unknowable forces of life which might, upon occasion, seize hold of individuals, drawing them out of their ordinary daytime roles and attitudes and restoring them to themselves, provided they had the courage to respond to the call and move under the shelter of the rainbow. The world war killed that faith in Lawrence; not his faith in life but his belief that either the ordinary people who put up with the values of modern society, or the privileged people who had made a conscious commitment to those values would remain alive in the "vital" sense. Nor could he believe any longer that exceptionally lively people might be able to alter that society from within. Early in *Women in Love* Birkin tells Gerald that people must either break up the present system or shrivel within it. By the end he realizes that the only breaking possible is to break and run for his life.

Women in Love, then, completes an entire cycle in the development of Lawrence's thinking and feeling as a novelist. Over a period of seven years he had learned how to construct a dazzlingly original narrative form through which "profound intuitions of life" could be brought to confront the systems of custom and convention, habit and law, work and art, thought and emotion determining the nature of social existence. But this lucid confrontation showed him only that there was no longer any common ground where life and history could meet, mingle, and enhance each other. In not one of the five novels he had left to write appears a single character like the young Ursula of *The Rainbow*, or Paul Morel, characters who run into the world with open arms and with the illusion that the societies into which they have been born can provide the conditions of vital freedom they seek.

Lawrence's novels of the early nineteen-twenties, written

hastily and in disregard of form, dominated by moods of anger, despair, revulsion, or indifference, reflect his recoil from the major constructive role he had gradually built up between the writing of the final version of *Sons and Lovers* and the final version of *Women in Love*. The two heroes of *Aaron's Rod* are men on the run with nowhere to run to, the one sickened by family life and the love of woman, the other concealing his lack of moral authority behind the brittle *persona* of an anti-democratic social prophet. The hero of *Kangaroo*, on the run from Europe toward the New World, plays with the idea of commitment either to a left-wing or to a quasi-fascistic social cause in Australia but finally continues his world tour with the self-disgusted realization that he simply does not care enough about people to involve himself.

The Plumed Serpent (1926) was written carefully in two successive drafts. Although Lawrence became deathly ill in the attempt to finish it while living in Mexico he pretended to himself for a time that it was his best novel. Clearly intended to set forth imaginatively a set of conditions under which men might recover their connection with the living universe, it managed to be the only cynical and heartless book Lawrence ever wrote. When the cult of Quetzalcoatl culminates in the blood bath at the church in Sayula, it becomes shatteringly clear that this hot world of dusky peons and mango trees is just as deathly as the industrial machine Gerald Crich had operated. Although Don Ramón preaches his boring sermons in the accents of Mr. Chadband, this idle, intensely vain hidalgo living on his wife's money and protected by a division of Mexican soldiers is more a rich thug in the tradition of the backers of *Algérie Française* and the plastic bomb terror than a mere crooked evangelist out of Dickens.

These three books represent Lawrence's hapless infatuation with notions of anti-democratic leadership. The two remaining novels, *The Lost Girl*, and more compellingly, *Lady Chatterley's Lover* (1928), show his attempt to generate a new world, replacing the ruined world described in *Women in Love*, out of a wholesome love affair between a man and a woman. Alvina Houghton and Cicio, Constance Chatterley and Mellors, continue the search begun by Ursula Brangwen and Birkin at the end of *Women in Love*. They are their heirs, so to speak. In both novels the motif of flight is central and poignant, and in both the sheer difficulty of the enterprise is not minimized. *The Lost Girl* ends with the lovers about to be separated by war, *Lady Chatterley* ends similarly in a separation.

Lawrence's lovers have wandered far in time from the light-drenched world of *The Rainbow* where life was a god speaking to men in the succession of seasons, in the sharp ecstasies of sensual communion, in the fruitions of child-bearing and old age, in the whirlwind seizures of death. They have even wandered far from the green slope facing the drab village where Paul and Miriam looked at flowers and practiced French together. But they possess their lives and loves intact, a kind of miracle Lawrence makes us believe in as he cannot begin to make us believe in Kangaroo's fatuous love gospel or the hot-gospeling of fat-thighed Don Ramón Quetzalcoatl.

PART III

THE BREAKING OF FORM

AARON'S ROD
KANGAROO
THE PLUMED SERPENT

1

$AARON'S\ ROD$ begins with the breaking of a blue Christmas tree ornament in the Sisson lower-middle-class home in the Midlands and substantially ends with the explosion of an anarchist's bomb in a Florentine café frequented by English remittance men. Among other things broken in the explosion is Aaron's flute which, along with a bowler hat, was one of the few things he carried with him on his flight from home, wife, and children. In a concluding chapter, Rawdon Lilly, a flower of the field who neither sews nor spins (although he does cook, clean, and darn), a latter-day Moses on the lookout for a priest, tells Aaron that his rod will flower again just as soon as he brings himself to recognize the reality of the power-urge and his own fate, which is to submit "to the heroic soul in a greater man." It goes without saying—because Lilly has already said it back in London—that the owner of the heroic soul is Lilly himself.

But the title of the last chapter is "Words." With pieces of broken flute in his hands and his sensitive musician's ears still ringing from the blast, Aaron seems indisposed to stir himself over Lilly's prosing about "the deep power-soul in the individual man." The modern reader, blessed with the superior insight of historical hindsight, is stirred in ways that Lawrence could not have anticipated. The bomb casually flung in the café announces an era of social chaos in Italy out of which will soon emerge a power-soul named Mussolini to elicit abject submission from all but the very rich. Furthermore, it is a kind of Viconian thunderclap ushering in two decades of savagery and folly which will see the rise of Nazism, the collapse of Russian socialism and of the League of Nations, the agony of Spain, the failure of democratic leadership in England and France, and the outbreak of a second world war. Lilly's slender claims to a knowledge of visionary truth are overwhelmed by a nightmare of history. His ethos of anarchic individualism and his insistence on the right to act in a spirit of pure irresponsibility lose their appeal when we see them written large in the revolution of nihilism engineered by master demolitionists like Hitler. Lilly's protest, to be heard, would have to sound in the middle of a settled era of bourgeois control. At the end of *Aaron's Rod* that era is finished for good.

Aaron Sisson's abrupt desertion of home for no "good" reason is an admirable way of beginning a critique of the customary forms by which people relate themselves to others and an exploration of possible alternate forms of relatedness. In *The Trespasser* Lawrence had written about a decent man driven to suicide by his own timorous acquiescence in a domestic situation gone bad. In *Sons and Lovers* he had shown Walter Morel sitting miserably in his shed at the bottom of the garden, with his bindle stiff on the coal pile, afraid to return to face his wife, equally afraid to strike out for freedom. The career of Sisson, a type of superior tramp and rogue male, is designed to compensate for these failures of masculine nerve. Aaron loves his wife and children, has an excellent if routine job, ready access to the randy landlady at the local pub, and a highly marketable talent for flute playing. Yet for him domesticity has come increasingly to represent the loss of a necessary self-possession. And so he sets forth in search of his own integrity and the blessed gift of a single selfhood in much the same way as one of the tramp saints of medieval Russia used to set out in search of his soul's salvation.

Aaron's Rod is a kind of Russian novel written for Anglo-Saxons, a novel in which the questions, "How should one live nowadays?" and "What must one do to be saved?" are kept constantly in view. The absurd love-fanatic Jim Bricknell, who "spent his time wavering about and going to meetings, philandering and weeping," is a wholly successful assimilation of a comic type out of Dostoevsky into Lawrence's art of portraiture; and the passionate involvement of the aged English tycoon Sir William Franks at Novara in questions of practical ethics recalls the passion for ethical debate that characterized Russian literature from Herzen to the Revolution and was, astonishingly, revived in the recent publication of *Doctor Zhivago*. Unfortunately, the power and authority of such a novel lie in the author's ability to suggest viable answers to his central questions or to suggest that his central characters are serious seekers after the living truth, however absurdly it may be formulated. But Lawrence's answers are not viable and his two main characters, Aaron and Lilly, lack ethical authenticity.

After leaving the Midlands Aaron is in search of a new center from which to live. Inevitably, he is offered the love of women, first Josephine Ford and later the Marchese Del Torre but recoils in the awareness that neither is interested in his integrity. The rod of Aaron's selfhood cannot flower in these affairs which merely repeat against a more glamorous social background the mode of connectedness he had experienced with his own wife and then rejected.

When he meets Lilly he is drawn to the man by his air of quiet authority and self-possession. Both are from exactly the same social class, even from the same English district, and both are equally anti-domestic. But the far more sophisticated and articulate Lilly has a defined ethical attitude which Aaron, adrift between the old life and an unforeseeable future, lacks. Lilly explains to Aaron something the latter feels to be true from his own experience: i.e., that the love urge, which has constituted the binding element of social and personal relations in the West has worn itself out and now leads to acts of violence and cruelty as people like Jim Bricknell attempt to keep the love game going through sheer willing. He also explains that there is a second great impulse, called the power urge, which it is time to employ in the reconstitution of personal and social relations. He suggests that a nucleus of relatedness in the mode of power would be the free submission of one man to the superior soul of a second, who would in turn pledge himself to respect the inferior's integrity; and he further suggests that Aaron might well want to make that submission to him.

Lilly's proposition to Aaron represents a critical juncture in the novel; and it is up to Lawrence to throttle the reader's (and Aaron's) natural skepticism by demonstrating the power-mode in action. He must find some way of dramatizing the hypothesis of an aristocracy based on intrinsic qualities of being in men so as to distinguish it from the forms of political, social, and personal tyranny that may be found everywhere in modern life. This is just what Lawrence does not get around to doing. Lilly badgers Aaron with advice that is sometimes sensible and sometimes foolish. When Aaron catches the flu he nurses him, when Aaron's bowels refuse to work properly, he saves his life by massaging him with linament. Yet none of these actions demonstrates the mode of power or suggests that Lilly is superior, intrinsically, to anyone else. Almost to the end of the novel Lilly remains an annoying little man, who may be refreshingly free from the duller middle-class shibboleths, but who is also unpleasantly self-conscious and humorless.

In the café scene terminated by the explosion of the bomb (pp. 267-273) Lilly loses entirely any claim to moral authority. He is sitting with Aaron, with an expatriate Scot of the upper-bohemian type named Argyle, and a "strange man: called Levinson." The conversation is about multiplying signs of social unrest in Italy, phenomena which the novel has already effectively documented through descriptions of a street riot in Milan and of a mysterious nighttime funeral cortege in Florence itself. Levinson, who is, one assumes, a Jew, attempts serious discussion and asks whether socialism is not the logical outcome of recent developments of European history. Aaron remains silent, Argyle, who is drunk, offers some heavily facetious remarks designed to make Levinson feel like an outsider; but it is left to Lilly to speak to the point, and his reply is thoroughly disgraceful.

The full debate is too lengthy to quote, but the salient parts can be summarized. Argyle has said that the world can be saved only through a revival of slavery of the Graeco-Roman type. He would make slaves of idealists, theorizing Jews, gentlemen, profiteers, Rothschilds, all politicians, the proletariat, and the professional classes. The level of thinking is perhaps only a little lower than one would expect from one sort of Englishman—or American for that matter—who hung about in Paris, Rome, Florence, or any of a dozen Mediterranean beach resorts during the nineteen-twenties, pretending to work but actually drinking and eating up an unearned income.

Levinson, belatedly recognizing Argyle for what he is, turns toward Lilly in search of more intelligible arguments. Lilly says: that socialism may be logically inevitable but he isn't interested; that all ideals, including love, liberty, fraternity, and the sanctity of human life, have gone putrid; that there must be a sort of slavery again because people are insects and instruments (he is close to Gerald Crich on this last point); that people can be brought to agree to their enslavement after "sufficient extermination" has been carried out among those who disagree; and that this "committal of the life issue of inferior beings to someone higher" can be secured by the exercise of military power. When Levinson asks him how serious he is he replies that he would say the opposite with equal fervor and adds that the one thing he hates is to see any living thing bullied. Since he and Argyle have been bullying Levinson throughout the conversation his name for insouciant inconsistency remains unblemished. And then the bomb goes off.

Despite the obvious parallels it would be a mistake to identify this colloquy of disaffected bourgeois intellectuals in an Italian café with similar colloquies held in the cafés of Munich, Vienna, and Berlin where disaffected bourgeois intellectuals like Rosenberg and Goebbels practiced the art of philosophico-politico dialectic before taking up careers in the world of *realpolitik* at the end of the decade. Argyle is merely a drunken ass and Lilly may be talking, as he often does, more to make a rhetorical *bella figura* than honestly. Besides, neither is a man of destiny. But the bomb, forcefully reminding us of the actual crisis Europe will enter in the nineteen-twenties, with such ghastly consequences in later decades, forces a harsher judgment. A pose of petulant nihilism colored with anti-Semitism struck at this particular time and place (northern Italy, 1920) is a blow struck against the living selves of all Europe. Lilly's bad will and bad faith in humanity are specifically political acts in this context and must be condemned out of hand.

If we cannot believe in Lilly's claims to intrinsic superiority, in his idea of power, and in his views of society, it becomes impossible to continue to take seriously Aaron's thirst after righteousness. On a hard view, and in the end the novel forces this view on all except the most incompetent of Lawrence's readers, Aaron, like the majority of the twenty thousand American men who take the option of a poor man's divorce each year, deserts his family simply out of boredom. He becomes a plaything of the idle rich, peddling his musical talent and sexual magnetism to neurotic upper-class wives and mistresses in exchange for more or less luxurious lodgings, fees, and sensations. He exploits the appetite of a jaded social set for queer birds and can be expected to go on drifting until his luck runs out with the onset of age and the decline of his novelty value. It is hard to imagine what he might be doing in twenty-five years' time. Perhaps if Italy continued to suit his indolent disposition he might be found improvising a musical background to speeches delivered over the Italian radio by Ezra Pound.

Most of *Kangaroo* was written in five weeks, during Lawrence's brief stay in Australia, where the story is set. Richard Aldington has described the writing as an "extraordinary *tour de force* of rapid composition, comparable with the almost fabulous creation of *Guy Mannering* in six weeks."[1] Lawrence himself took a less generous view, referring to the book as "wild," "a queer show," "a funny sort of novel where nothing happens and such a lot of things should happen."[2] One thing that ought to have happened was correction of the several hundred typographical errors which have remained in the text since it was first printed. *Kangaroo* is the most padded and redundant of Lawrence's novels. He is careful to describe at length the appearance and furnishing of rooms in which no dramatic scenes take place,

[1] In his introduction to the Phoenix Edition of *Kangaroo* (London: Heinemann, 1955), vii.

[2] See *The Collected Letters of D. H. Lawrence*, ed. Harry T. Moore (New York: Viking, 1962), II, 708.

to inventory the distant relatives of intolerably minor characters. From a formal point of view, the book is a heap of bits and fragments blown about on air currents of emotion. By expressing the vagaries of Lawrence's thinking and feeling at a peculiarly distressed time of his life in a shapeless, wandering narrative it offers one of the lengthiest, if not one of the most powerful, challenges to the argument for the fallaciousness of imitative form since Rousseau's *Confessions*.

The story is narrowly focused on the English writer Richard Lovat Somers and its *donné* is Somers' extreme unhappiness and disorientation as he reaches the end of early manhood and looks ahead to middle age. For Somers a visit to Australia coincides with a mild crisis in his marriage, an acute crisis in his relations to political society, and a crisis of "volcanic" scale in his feelings toward mankind *en bloc*. These problems overlap and interweave throughout the story as told. Lovat's interest in the Diggers and in the socialist labor leader Willie Struthers is stimulated partly by his idea that he must make a place for himself in the man's world to counterbalance his uxorious interest in Harriet Somers. His disenchantment with mankind influences his decision not to be recruited by either the Socialists or the Diggers.

When Lovat leaves Australia "over a cold, dark, inhospitable sea" none of these problems has been settled, except in terms of subjective emotional reactions of a negative sort. He is still with Harriet but remains as isolated from the man's world as Will Brangwen ever was. He has ended his flirtation with Ben Cooley (that is, Kangaroo) and turned down the labor leader's proposition, but only because he thinks it is his fate to remain disengaged from all social movements—not from any clear understanding that one of the movements is viciously corrupt. He has connected his overt misanthropy—his preference for the emptiness of the Australian bush and the inhumanness of the salt sea to human society—with the humiliation and persecution he and his wife had suffered at the hands of jingoistic English officials during the war. But he has not learned to forgive men in general for the misdeeds of one group of men. Although admitting that the war and the draft were necessary, that the security regulations which had driven him and Harriet from Cornwall were also necessary, he feels in his soul an undying hatred and suspicion, and a final indifference to even the minimum claims that the organized human collectivity must levy on the individual.

The most unsettling thing about *Kangaroo* is that it ends where most serious novels would begin. Its answer to the perennial moral imperative of novelists—"Only connect"—is a loud "No." Lawrence refuses to connect his sense of personal hurt with a thoughtful account of actual social conditions in Australia. He hugs his wound and consequently fails to illuminate his main subject, which I take to be the same as Conrad's in *Under Western Eyes*: namely, the tragic question of the relation of private values to large public issues during a period of acute political crisis.

The trouble in Lovat's marriage is precipitated largely through his rather schematic notions about what marriage can be. According to him, marriages are one of three types: (a) in which the husband is lord and master; (b) in which the husband is the perfect lover; (c) in which the husband is the true friend and companion. He feels he has enjoyed (b) with Harriet yet is convinced that "a marriage of the perfect-lover type is bound either to end in catastrophe or to slide away toward (a) or (c)," after the first years. He would like his own marriage to resolve itself into (a) but is willing to settle for (c) in the face of his wife's jeering dismissal of the lord and master idea.

In addition, Lovat is suffering from an occupational disease of authors. The nature of his work keeps him at home under his wife's eye. Harriet is satisfied enough but Lovat has come to identify masculinity itself with getting out of the house and into some active role in public life. He has the nostalgia for power that sometimes afflicts intellectuals who believe they have good ideas yet never see these ideas put into practice. Shortly before leaving Europe he had written some essays attacking democracy. The fact that these writings have caused some stir has fostered in him the illusion that he may be able to stir things up by becoming a leader of men instead of merely continuing to set words on paper while sitting at the kitchen table.

Under these circumstances he is ripe for the blandishments of the weird would-be dictator, Kangaroo, and willing to lend at least half an ear to Struthers' suggestion that he join the Australian Socialist movement. He denies Struthers rather abruptly on the defensible ground that socialism, by expressing the basic relation of working-class people as a cash nexus, perpetuates the ideology of the very social system it is attempting to dismantle. Kangaroo preaches the love-ideal as a new social principle which will save Australia from decadence through the love of male "mates" for one another. At the level of political action he has articulated this astonishing principle in the Diggers, an association of "athletic clubs" where petty bourgeois war veterans sworn to unquestioning obedience are systematically indoctrinated in hate and instructed in the terrorist arts of assassination with knife, pistol, and iron bar. Kangaroo peddles his doctrine to Somers in an intensely personal way, over magnificent lunches with wine and to the accompaniment of a good deal of touching and ogling. This tender would-be fuehrer from down under makes nothing of the shattering contradiction between his declared ideals and the nauseous reality of the fascistic movement he leads.

All this is presented by Lawrence without detectable irony, or with an irony so self-lacerating as to pass for partial assent to the particular version of Double-Think (hate equals love; mateyness condones murder of one's fellow citizens, especially if they are trade-unionists) which the Digger movement embodies. Through his friendship with Jack Callcott, one of Kangaroo's underlings, Somers is privy early on to the destructive methods and illegal objectives of the movement. Nevertheless, when he should be running up the street after a policeman he prefers to go on arguing a case for phallicism and the dark gods of the lower body against the woozy idealism of Kangaroo.

A showdown is reached at a strike meeting where Carruthers speaks, rather ineptly, on the wage question, until Callcott and his goons precipitate a bloody brawl. A bomb is thrown, Kangaroo is wounded in the stomach, and Callcott smashes the skulls of three men with an iron bar, reporting afterward to Somers that

". . . the best of it is . . . you feel a perfect *angel* after it. You don't feel you've done any harm. Feel as gentle as a lamb all round. I can go to Victoria, now, and be as gentle —" He jerked his head in the direction of Victoria's room. "And you bet she'll like me."

His eyes glowed with a sort of exaltation.

"Killing's natural to a man, you know," he said. "It is just as natural as lying with a woman. Don't you think?"

And still Richard did not answer.   (pp. 326-327)

At the end of this scene the narrator remarks that it was curious no one brought criminal charges against anybody but fails to explain why Somers, who is in the best position to help the police, did not do so; or why in fact he has no answer to make to Jack's pathological revelations. The appalling fact is that Somers is too busy exploring his emotional reaction to the scene of violence he witnessed to do or say anything whatsoever. Furthermore, he goes on seeing members of the Diggers until he leaves Australia, even remaining in touch with the unspeakable Callcott.

Somers' detachment, like Rawdon Lilly's, comes in the end to resemble in every detail a state of moral bankruptcy. His principle of *non serviam*, because it is combined with a thorough lack of self-discipline and a defective sense of reality, causes him to serve as an accessory after the fact to capital crime. Also, it is not too much to say that Somers acts consistently in bad faith. He enters into relations with extremist elements of Australian society within a few days of coming to the country and without any knowledge of objective social and political conditions beyond what he has picked up from reading the morning papers. From the beginning of his association with Kangaroo he lets the man think he may be able to commit himself eventually to the movement when he knows full well that he will never commit himself. Finally, he has left Europe because of the bullying he endured in England during the war, but can find nothing better to do in Australia than carry on a flirtation with a group of political bullies; that is, apart from sea bathing and strolls through the countryside behind the South Coast.

One hesitates to call Somers a blockhead, yet he is certainly one of those revolutionary simpletons whom Wyndham Lewis first categorized in discussing the case of Ezra Pound. Somers wanders through the modern world, obeying the dictates of feelings which arise from a wounded sensibility. The consequences of this sort of self-indulgence, from the standpoint of intelligence, sincerity, and humanity, are such as would make an angel weep. This is the obvious lesson that *Kangaroo* teaches: fear tyranny but fear equally the man of extreme sensibility who involves himself

in social questions while refusing to bring critical intelligence to bear on the real nature of the issues. Unfortunately, so far as one can tell from the novel itself and from
Lawrence's few comments on it, the lesson was unintended.
Fortunately, Lawrence did set down a principle by which
the lesson may be extracted without the author's permission.
"Never trust the artist, trust the tale."

The didactic theme of *The Plumed Serpent* is expressed
by the narrator in one of his many editorial comments on
the story he tells:

> That which is aboriginal in America still belongs to the way
> of the world before the Flood, before the mental-spiritual
> world came into being. In America, therefore, the mental-
> spiritual life of white people suddenly flourishes like a great
> weed let loose in virgin soil. Probably it will as quickly
> wither. A great death come. And after that, the living result
> will be a new germ, a new conception of human life, that
> will arise from the fusion of the old blood-and-vertebrate
> consciousness with the white man's present mental-spiritual
> consciousness. The sinking of both beings into a new being.
> (p. 413)

This theme is articulated in two ways. Kate Leslie, a "mental-spiritual" representative of European culture, meets with
Cipriano, a dark full-blooded Mexican Indian, and after
considerable soul-searching and vacillation agrees to marry
him. The second embodiment of the theme is in the central
action, which consists of the successful attempt of Don
Ramón Carrasco, a Mexican of pure Spanish stock acting

in conjunction with Cipriano, to drive Christianity from Mexico, putting in its place a revived worship of the ancient Aztec gods. The separate versions of the theme become one when Kate is invited to join the newly formed pantheon of Aztec deities as the goddess Malintzi, humble consort of the war god Huitzilopochtli, *i.e.*, Cipriano. The novel ends with her "sinking" and a good bit short of describing the "new being" her gesture may help create.

Once under way, after some brilliantly projected scenes in Mexico City and a long account in Lawrence's best descriptive manner of Kate's journey to Sayula on Lake Chapala, the novel moves ahead as an alternation between the heroine's soul-searching and accounts of solemn rituals celebrating the return of the chief god Quetzalcoatl to his unhappy people. Features of these rituals include a series of hymns which set forth in highly allusive, metaphorical language the principal tenets of the cult, special symbolic emblems, gestures, and ceremonies. Don Ramón, who is as fond of *outré* costumes and flummery as an American Shriner, keeps an entire guild of weavers and dyers busy in his hacienda turning out ceremonial garments. Where the money for these elegant materials comes from is a minor mystery. However, any reader with even an elementary grounding in economics knows that in the end it must come from the peons whose way of life the cult is intended to revitalize.

Lawrence drew on his wide reading in anthropology, theosophy, and the history of New World religions to provide spectacular details of the cult practices. The essence of the religion is described as a worship of the opposed principles of earth and sky. The central emblem of Quetzalcoatl consists of an eagle clutching an encircling serpent. The symbolism is of simultaneous opposition and interdependence between the two principles. This image of dualism, whether genuinely Aztec or purely Laurentian, recalls both the lion-unicorn opposition of "The Crown" and the function of the rainbow arch as symbol in *The Rainbow*.

Much as the reader may sympathize with Kate's cry early in the novel—"Give me the mystery and let the world live again for me! And deliver me from man's automatism"—he cannot discover any significant mystery embodied in the occasionally picturesque but usually bathetic rituals of *The Plumed Serpent*. To the religious and skeptic alike the hymns and ceremonies Lawrence has designed must seem a supreme example of pseudo-reference. They point toward nothing. We are told that the Mexican masses live anew once the decadent worship of Christ and His mother has been banished from their churches, but signs of renewed vigor are few indeed. At the end of the novel the nation is embroiled in bloody civil and religious war. For Mexico there is nothing new in that.

In *Fantasia of the Unconscious*, an eccentric treatise published shortly before *Kangaroo*, Lawrence had written:

> For the mass of people, knowledge *must* be symbolical, mythical, dynamic. This means you must have a higher, responsible, conscious class: and then in varying degrees the lower classes, varying in their degree of unconsciousness. Symbols must be true from top to bottom. But the interpretation of the symbols must rest, degree after degree, in the higher, responsible, conscious classes.[3]

Elsewhere in the same book Lawrence recommends total illiteracy for the lower classes. This leaves us with the image of a society in which a ruling class controls the responses of the masses by controlling and dictating the symbols to which these ignorant masses give unconscious and inevitable obedience. Whether this "conscious" class were a

---

[3] *Fantasia*, p. 99.

priesthood, a military clique, or a dictator's ministers, it would be in a position to become absolutely corrupted in the enjoyment of absolute power.

The Plumed Serpent directly translates these ideas into fiction. Don Ramón, and Cipriano in his less conscious degree, create a semi-priestly, semi-military dictatorship. They hold power by waving the symbols of the Quetzalcoatl cult before the dazed eyes of the Mexican masses. When they are betrayed by disloyal followers, they do not attempt to re-examine the adequacy of the "true symbols." Instead they carry out a ritualistic blood-bath in which they offer the spectacle of their own cruelty to their obedient flock as an ineffable symbol of truth.

Nor does Don Ramón bear much looking into as the novel's chief representative of a "higher, responsible, conscious class," whether we concentrate on his crude treatment of his first wife, his outstanding lack of success as a landed proprietor before he hit upon the notion of making a good thing out of his country's ancient traditions, his compulsive exhibitionism, his essentially psychotic ability to improvise techniques of meditation through which he can reach the state of trance he requires for decision-making, the artsy-craftsiness of his taste in ceremonial serapes, his cynicism, his hysterical ability to believe his own lies and to become himself hypnotized by the hypnotic techniques he employs to influence his followers. Don Ramón on one occasion shows great physical courage, but this trait is not unknown among Mexican bandits. And even if he were brave *and* good the sheer banality of his liturgical style would compel complete dissent from his principles. One example, happily, will suffice:

> Who sleeps—shall wake! Who sleeps—shall wake! Who treads down the path of the snake shall arrive at the place; in the path of the dust shall arrive at the place and be dressed in the skin of the snake.   (p. 172)

Kate Leslie has arrived nerve-worn in Mexico at the age of about forty with two marriages and much experience of the mental-spiritual sort behind her. She may well desire to throw the rest of her life away and sink into a state of benumbed mindlessness. In any case, she is offered a position at the top of the new social-religious order, and part of her marriage bargain with Cipriano is that she shall be allowed vacations in Europe as often and for as long as she wants. But Kate's future is not, after all, the chief point. Unless one is prepared to write off Quetzalcoatlism as a mere tourist attraction one must ask what it intends to do for the peons, to whom Don Ramón addresses the overwhelming proportion of his prodigious output of flyers and propaganda leaflets. On the novel's own showing the Mexican Indian is sunk in ignorance and apathy, exploited by landlords, terrorized by bloodthirsty bandits, brainwashed by Catholic clergymen from the pulpits of the thousands of Mexico's churches. The Indian needs food, housing, knowledge, fair treatment, and a new sense of purpose in his life. How does the new order intend to meet these needs? In a word, by leaving the Indian hungry and ignorant, by permitting the exploitation of landlords to continue, by the terror of Cipriano's bandit troops, by using the thousands of Mexico's churches as Aztec temples where blood sacrifices of Indian men and women are carried out. Only this time it is called "a new vision of the living universe."

In these books Lawrence retreats from the ideal of a vital freedom which had been the animating principle of his earlier novels. If we assume that he endorses the actions and values of a Rawdon Lilly, a Richard Somers, a living

Quetzalcoatl, we shall have to accuse him of sheer sophis-
try, of making the worse appear the better part. Yet this
conclusion somehow appears too simple. All three of these
novels have a disconcerting way of turning on themselves,
of suddenly and suspiciously resembling satires of the very
persons and ideas that are being held up for admiration.
After all, it is Lawrence's own hand which flings the bomb
into the café to break up Lilly's vapid pose of disaffiliation;
and of Somers Lawrence can write so finally deflating a comment as this: "As a poet, he felt himself entitled to all kinds
of emotions and sensations which an ordinary man would
have repudiated."

If Lawrence never openly repudiates the bathos of the
neo-Aztec revival it is hard to believe that there is not a
grim humor at work as we watch the insane proliferation
of ritual detail in the final third of *The Plumed Serpent*.
The tone of many episodes in *Aaron's Rod* and *Kangaroo* is
mocking, even jeering. After congratulating ourselves for
having seen through the leadership ideal in its three successive versions, we ought possibly to suspect that we have
only done what the author wished.

Again, *that* conclusion is too simple. These books are not
works of ironic duplicity, subtly undermining their own apparent preachments. The laughter one may choose to hear
echoing through even so solemn a production as *The
Plumed Serpent* is desperate, not confidently ironic. In
Aaron, Lilly, Somers, and Kate as well, Lawrence draws
partial portraits of himself, as every reader knows. When
these characters are mocked at, Lawrence undermines himself. Don Ramón is permitted not only to say and do stupid,
cruel things, but also to speak on behalf of ideas in which
Lawrence passionately believed. To permit a murderer to
call men to a new vision of the living universe was for Lawrence a fundamental self-betrayal.

The leadership novels reflect a temporary breakdown in Lawrence's morale, a semi-deliberate giving way to confusion. In each book Lawrence demonstrates an acute political insight which he then proceeds to subvert. *Aaron's Rod* is one of the first novels of its period to express a characteristic aspect of the nineteen-twenties—the widespread feeling of rootlessness and *anomie*—and to grasp intuitively a connection between that feeling and the emergence in the West of an era of nihilism. Yet Aaron and Lilly, both exactly typifying what has gone wrong with the age, are exactly the wrong people through whom to bring the age to judgment. When Lawrence shows the movement Kangaroo leads to be a blend of poisonous, homoerotic sentimentalism, and crude violence he uncovers a fundamental truth about the nature of all fascist movements. Yet Somers, who is himself poisonously sentimental, potentially homoerotic, and preyed upon by impulses of crude violence, merely embarrasses Lawrence's genuine insights. Given the extraordinary mixture of pagan and Catholic elements in Mexican post-Colonial religious practices, Lawrence's idea of an Aztec restoration engineered by persons seeking to replace the country's social revolution by a conservative dictatorship is nothing short of inspired. Yet his pretense that this outcome is anything but a human catastrophe makes the heart sink.

How can we account for the collapse of morale, the very real loss of moral focus these novels show? We know that Lawrence had suffered an enormous disillusionment as he was harried about from London to Cornwall to Berkshire to the Midlands and back to London by the thought police of England's civil defense apparatus in the later years of the war. His shock reaction, which is fully and painfully described in the famous "Nightmare" chapter of *Kangaroo*, was probably intensified by the barbarous treatment inflicted on his two best novels. *The Rainbow*, published in 1915, was suppressed within a few days by an order from the Home Office. *Women in Love* was ready for publication in November 1916, but could not be issued at all until 1920 and then only in a private edition. Novels are written to be read. These mean suppressions undoubtedly eroded Lawrence's faith that he had an audience, especially an English audience. Whereas *Sons and Lovers* or *Women in Love* are patently addressed to English people, the leadership group seems directed primarily toward the anomic, professionally disenchanted types Lawrence was forced to meet and know as he drifted about in Italy, Germany, Ceylon, Australia, New Mexico, and Mexico from 1919 onward. The chief characters of these novels are, overwhelmingly, self-exiles from the European bourgeoisie who fall into positions of political and social extremism from despair at finding anything tenable to cling to. The same formula may cover Lawrence himself during some of those years.

PART IV

THE DEED OF LIFE

THE LOST GIRL
LADY CHATTERLEY'S LOVER

1

IN 1916, LAWRENCE tried to get a manuscript-in-prog-
ress called *The Insurrection of Miss Houghton* from his
wife's German relatives. Under wartime conditions this
proved impossible, and he was not to have the opportunity
of continuing the book, which was finally issued as *The
Lost Girl* (1920), until the war's end. Begun before *The
Rainbow* and completed just before he became immersed in
the leadership theme, *The Lost Girl* underlines the fact
that the work of major novelists rarely follows a tidy
chronological pattern of development and is often full of
remarkable anticipations and odd transpositions, of haunting
déja vues and equally haunting adumbrations. When we
come to know the life-work of a great writer we are apt
to find ourselves brooding about the unknown masterpiece
he did not live to write. But there is a sense—not altogether
mystical, one hopes—in which this masterpiece is alive and
written on every page from first to last, creating a composition of the whole, a Jamesian carpet-figure, that the
most considered criticism is powerless to elicit.

The Lost Girl and *Lady Chatterley's Lover*, separated in
their publication dates by an interval of eight years, are
closely related thematically and with respect to their central dramatic movement. In the ninth chapter of *Lady Chatterley* Lawrence wrote a statement about fiction which helps
to define this movement:

> And here lies the vast importance of the novel, properly
> handled. It can inform and lead into new places the flow
> of our sympathetic consciousness, and it can lead our sym-
> pathy away in recoil from things gone dead.

While this famous passage is overtly concerned with the
relation of a novel to its readers, it also precisely describes

both the outer and inner action of *The Lost Girl* and of *Lady Chatterley*. With the former novel the recoil is from a Midland town called Woodhouse, and the new place is a wild district of the Abruzzi mountains in Italy. In the latter novel the recoil is from Wragby Hall and the industrial village of Tevershall, while the new place is Wragby Wood, a fragment of forest lying between the village and the manor house. Yet these new places prove less than adequate on the literal plane as alternatives to the things gone dead from which the characters take their departure. Residence in Italy fails to solve a single one of the severe problems faced by Alvina and Cicio as newlyweds anticipating the birth of their first child in wartime. Similarly, the wood where Connie and Mellors become acquainted and make love provides at best a meager and temporary hiding place from a surrounding world which refuses to become well lost.

Nevertheless, as soon as one considers the inner significance of these "places," they are seen to retain full power to render Lawrence's constructive vision. For, fundamentally, both Italy and Wragby Wood are images of a change of heart and a redirection of consciousness to which Alvina and Connie submit in the experience of passionate love. Since there can be no guarantee, in a world full of dead things, that the heroines will never regress toward deadness, there must be an inevitable, ironic discrepancy between the literal and mythic significance of Lawrence's new places. To the extent that Lady Chatterley, as we shall see that she does a little later, fuses herself with the wood and carries its vital principle deep inside her, the wood is "sacred" and inviolable—unless and until she ceases to stand by the difficult choice her affair with Mellors represents. And yet the "real" wood is moribund and is about to give way to housing estates for miners and factory workers. Similarly, the "real" Italy is merely a more brutal and colorful part of civilized Europe than Woodhouse, but as long as Alvina remains with Cicio she is in the Italy of Lawrence's vision.

It was pointed out at the beginning of Part II that early in his career Lawrence faced an anguish of combining his sense of life with what he saw as the dead shell of social and historical actuality; and it was asserted that he would be tempted in this anguish to recoil into despair and nay-saying, or to slide off toward the pastoral simplification suggested by "figures in a landscape in true proportion." Now if *The Lost Girl* and *Lady Chatterley* dramatize a recoil from dead things, and if these books are in any way describable as pastoral—as I believe they are—need we assume they demonstrate a failure of faith and nerve like the failure of those novels we considered in the previous chapter?

The answer to my rhetorical question is, "Certainly not!" The leadership books show a mood of angry disillusionment and of ambitiousness gone sour. By contrast, in *Lady Chatterley* and, to a lesser degree, *The Lost Girl*, the strategic withdrawal of the principal characters from the moribund world requires courage, cunning, endurance, and an unimpaired will. These lovers have first to create or recreate their own freedom before the prison doors fly open. The redirection of consciousness is a process which, like Being itself, has no termination short of actual physical death. It is hard, moral work, pursued in a landscape strewn with the wrecked hopes of a dying culture.

As pastorals these novels seem classically conformable to William Empson's inspired axiom about putting the complex into the simple, with the corollary that the complex is not itself simplified thereby but rather is illuminated from a new perspective.[1] What is complex is Lawrence's

[1] See William Empson, *English Pastoral Poetry* (New York: W. W. Norton, 1938), p. 23.

sense of the crisis which Western society as a whole is under-going. We sense this crisis in the predispositions of both sets of lovers at the beginning of their love affairs and in the many references to war and the insensate industrial climate. The simple is the fundamental rhythm of human passion to which the lovers gradually surrender their despair and cynicism. Lawrence does not explain how we are to "journey across" from contemplation of a lover's flow of sympathetic consciousness to the transformation of a society, but society begins and ends with private persons and there is more than a half truth in the notion that the problem of the Many is the problem of the Few multiplied.

The thing most valuable and moving in these books for the present time is Lawrence's absolute insistence that the experience which is wholly private and personal should not be submerged and lost in the tumult of public catastrophe or sacrificed to any set of merely general standards. Clifford Chatterley hates Connie not because she sleeps with a servant but because in seeking to marry Mellors she refuses to acknowledge an impersonal obligation to her class position as mistress of Wragby. When Cicio is signing his passport in the Italian Consulate, Alvina disrupts the bureaucratic rhythm by bending to kiss his moving hand, and when Cicio meets his friend Geoffrey in the Gare de Lyon during the first weeks of the war, the two men, instead of stiffening their upper lips, weep tears of despair on each other's shoulders. The art of *The Lost Girl* and of *Lady Chatterley's Lover* is designed to establish the authority of the private experience and the essential human rhythm *against* the authority of the merely public and the insensate rhythms of our machine civilization.

2

The action of *The Lost Girl* may be characterized by combining the adjective of the title phrase with a gerund. The novel dramatizes becoming lost and shows that for the heroine, Alvina Houghton, the experience merges with an experience of becoming found. One may recognize in this formula a secular variant of a central Christian paradox. In Christianity the paradox is sustained on the assumption that man, a duality of body and soul, is of necessity twice born, once into mortal and once into immortal life. Lawrence's paradox also rests on an assumption of dualism. His two terms are two selves coexistent within the human subject, the "higher" self of moral, intellectual, and social awareness, and the "lower" self of physical instinct; or, as it is put by a homely bit of punning imagery early in the novel, two sides of a coin—the head and the tail. Alvina becomes lost by choosing to renounce the higher self and to embrace a destiny which is mainly instinctual. When in the middle of the story she descends into an "atavistic" darkness of sexual thralldom to her animal-like Italian lover, she is, in terms of conventional morality, a lost girl indeed. But from another perspective she has now discovered her "real self" and can anticipate fulfillment.

This formula actually inverts the Christian paradox inasmuch as Alvina dies out of a condition of spinsterish and self-renunciatory high-mindedness and is reborn flesh, just as Lawrence's claim for the superiority of "blood-consciousness" to mental consciousness[2] inverts those traditional as-

[2] Some important documents in which Lawrence sets forth this claim are: a famous letter to Ernest Collings written in 1913 ("my great religion is a belief in the blood, the flesh, as being wiser than the intellect")—see *Letters*, pp. 96-97 for the full credo; his rather cranky

sumptions of Western ethics which stress the superiority of mind and insist that the claims of instinct are to be denied or, at least, kept rigorously controlled. In keeping with this pattern of inversion, it can be shown that the entire novel is structured in terms of the idea of descent, of movement downward into a rich, shapeless darkness. Whether one views Alvina realistically or as the protagonist of a symbolic drama, it remains true that she extricates herself from drab circumstances not by rising above, but by sinking below them. *The Lost Girl* celebrates the triumph of low-mindedness and attempts to replace the old metaphors of moral strenuousness which fixed moral achievement in expressions like "higher laws," "ascendency," "superiority," "uplift," and so forth with fresh metaphors of downward-ness and underneathness.

Early in the novel we are told that since in Alvina high-mindedness was stretched beyond the breaking point, she must go right back on it in order to survive. The narrator then denies that in so doing Alvina betrays her higher self and illustrates his point with the image of the coin:

> If we turn over the head of the penny and look at the tail, we don't thereby deny or betray the head. We do but adjust it to its own complement. . . .
>
> So Alvina spun her medal, and her medal came down tails.   (pp. 34-35)

This emphasis is worth bearing in mind when we consider the representative or argumentative character of the book. Lawrence's intention is to readjust to each other two complementary sides of the human character which have broken asunder under the strains imposed by social convention and

correspondence with Bertrand Russell during the first world war—see Harry T. Moore, "D. H. Lawrence's Letters to Bertrand Russell," *Atlantic Monthly*, December 1948, pp. 100-101; *Fantasia of the Unconscious* (1922).

a one-sided moral tradition. There is no argument against "spiritual" values as such, only the assumption that it is impossible to establish a "high" civilization on a foundation of repressed and devitalized instinctive experience.

It will be useful to review Alvina's downward career from the approximate standpoint of the conventional British middle-class social ethic, vintage 1913. 1913 is the year she escapes from the Midlands to Italy. She is born the daughter of a respectable though quixotic clothier who moves steadily toward financial ruin throughout the first third of the novel. Until well into her twenties she behaves in exemplary conformity to the mores of her family and community, and might look forward to marriage with a social equal recruited from one of Woodhouse's business families. However she avoids this fate without ever entering into open revolt against the community. Her tactic of avoidance develops slowly and is helped along by circumstances beyond her control, mainly by her father's successive bankruptcies. Its principal feature is her steady and eventually complete loss of caste in the eyes of the community.

First, she refuses appropriate suitors and drops down from the category of marriageable virgin into the contemptible category of old maid. Second, she deliberately "vulgarizes" herself by taking up the low profession of nurse-midwife. Third, she totally loses middle-class respectability by consorting with the shabby troupers of James Houghton's vaudeville theatre. Fourth, she proves herself beneath contempt by becoming the mistress of a member of a vaudeville troupe. Fifth, she vanishes from sight to become the abjectly submissive wife of an impoverished Italian peasant. From first to last Alvina sinks slowly to the bottom of society and by the end has become a creature more to be pitied than censured, a sad case; or, as the magnanimous Dr. Mitchell put it in his letter to her:

So your fair-seeming face covered the schemes and vices
of your true nature. Well, I can only thank Providence
which spared me the disgust and shame of marrying you,
and I hope that, when I meet you on the streets of Leicester
Square, I shall have forgiven you sufficiently to be able to
throw you a coin.   (p. 339)

Against this communal interpretation of Alvina's career
we have only to place the evaluation suggested by Lawrence's symbols and narrative point of view to appreciate
the total transformation of conventional tribal morality
which this novel undertakes. In these terms Alvina's career
is an arduous and impeded yet triumphant descent from
death to life. A healthy instinct makes her sink beneath the
town's height of respectability. By so doing she escapes the
living death of a worn-out family tradition, best symbolized
in the invalid mother with her neurotic heart disease, escapes Woodhouse with its name suggestive of coffins, and
escapes England, last seen from the middle of the Channel
as a "long, ash-grey coffin slowly emerging." And it must
be emphasized that we are asked to interpret this flight as
a moral achievement.

For the modern reader the assumption of the intrinsic
morality of human instinct is difficult to allow. The reader
who is too sophisticated to support the communal judgment
on Alvina's case may, on the other hand, want to dispense
with moral distinctions altogether and view Alvina either
cynically, sentimentally, or from the broadly amoral perspective supplied by the naturalism of a Dreiser or a Zola.
But this will not work, because Lawrence's naturalism is
ethical: natural instincts are neither evil nor amoral; they
are potentially good. Alvina is not a Sister Carrie, nor for
that matter a Sophia Baines. Rather, she is the obverse of
the figure of a medieval lady who withdraws from the social world by taking the veil and spends the rest of her days

in arduous spiritual exercises. (Along these lines, an appropriate image for Alvina is one suggested in the latter part of the novel: "She felt herself like one of the old sacred prostitutes: a sacred prostitute.")

Another kind of difficulty faced by the reader in allowing Lawrence's claim that Alvina's choice is moral is that, in fact, choice does not seem to enter in at all. We are told that "there was an inflexible fate within her, which shaped her ends." And we hear that

> fate had been too strong for her and her desires: fate which
> was not an external association of forces, but which was
> integral in her own nature. Her own inscrutable nature
> was her fate: sore against her will.   (pp. 39-40)

To reinvoke the Christian nun, we seem here to be dealing with something analogous to a religious vocation. Something in Alvina chooses for her even as God chooses for the nun. Choice, since it originates in a part of her nature which is inscrutable, cannot be directly investigated with an eye to valuing the motivations behind it, but it can be dramatized as a process in conflict with the impediments of her conventional social will. Furthermore, if one does not insist on free choice as a condition of moral action—and pure free choice is seen to be a fiction as soon as we recognize that individuals are never entirely free from both internal and external pressures to which they are continuously responding for as long as they live—then the question of the morality of Alvina's action remains open.

To explore Lawrence's redefinition of traditional social morality and to allow it to assert its claims against the tribal ethic, we need now to look at a detailed pattern of symbolism through which this redefinition is mainly expressed. For *The Lost Girl* does not argue a case discursively. Instead it presents a submerged pattern of meanings through a variety of symbolic devices and techniques, and it is only by inspection of the symbols that one can determine how effectively Lawrence's "descendentalist" outlook illuminates the problems of experience raised in the novel.

The word "darkness," which has already been made use of several times in this chapter, is the key term in the symbolism of *The Lost Girl*. Broadly speaking, darkness designates the stratum of instinct within the self which is ordinarily overlaid by moral, psychological, and social conditioning, and crushed into submission by high-mindedness. Matching the heroine's slow descent toward instinctual expression is a countermovement in the novel, best described as the empowering of darkness or the freeing of instinct from its cultural prison. *The Lost Girl* does not portray a revolution from beneath in which the forces of darkness overrun the social forces of light, although in one extraordinary passage it envisions just such a revolution. Lawrence was too well aware of the tremendous handicaps under which natural instincts operate in modern culture to attempt to sustain anything of the sort. But as an artist working in necessarily dramatic materials, he found it necessary to give darkness an objective embodiment. The instinct within Alvina had to be answered from without. She could not make the downward journey alone, and she required cues to direct her toward her obscure destination.

For Ursula the demands of instinct were bodied forth in a herd of horses, but this was perhaps an hallucinatory projection of inner conflict; when the hallucination passed, she was left with no clear idea of where she could turn. The symbols of instinct both as value and as a self-sustaining mode of experience are more varied, more concrete, less peripheral in *The Lost Girl*. They range from slight foreshadowings to things as palpable and gross as a tattooed man, a coal mine, an Italian. In order to show the development of the symbolism of darkness in *The Lost Girl* it will be useful to consider it under the following headings: *Foreshadowings; Cicio as Symbol; Italy as Symbol.*

FORESHADOWINGS

The Lost Girl is, for more than one-third of its length, the story of an old maid. Yet Alvina is reserved for an extraordinary, inevitable fate, and so it becomes the narrator's problem to suggest from the beginning the secret presence of this fate, even while Alvina is caught in the toils of high-mindedness and is years away from a conscious decision to become lost. Lawrence makes heavy use of the traditional literary device of foreshadowing to create this suggestion.

As early as the second chapter, with its ironic title, "The Rise of Alvina Houghton," the reader is given hints of the dark self lurking in the heroine and is shown a representative situation in which the hidden impulses of her nature are answered, as it were, by an intruder who appears briefly within the stuffy little world of Woodhouse and then vanishes. This slim, blue-eyed, and demure girl, raised by the devoted and wholly high-minded Miss Frost, is intermittently subject to peculiar moods of jeering hilarity. At such times, to the eye of her distressed companion her face takes on a "gargoyle look," and there is an "odd, derisive look at the back of her eyes, a look of old knowledge and deliberate derision." Alvina is unconscious of these subversive traits in her character, although they frighten away the conventional young men of the community. Therefore she is unprepared to respond to the challenge posed by her first fiancé, Dr. Alexander Graham. Nevertheless, the mere fact that this strange man is her first lover prepares her, and the reader, for her ultimate break with the "daylight" world; for Graham is the first human embodiment of darkness presented for our inspection and he is a direct foreshadowing of Cicio.

Graham, an Australian, "dark in coloring, with very dark eyes, and a body which seemed to move inside his clothing," with a "strong mouthful of cruel, compact teeth," is hardly a character in the conventional sense. He is more an emblem of the lower self, just as Miss Frost is a more or less pure representative of the higher self. He creates for Alvina the possibility of experience in opposition to the modes of being and knowing available in Woodhouse, and, by extension, in all England. When Alvina dallies with Graham during their engagement, her voice takes on "a curious bronze-like resonance" and she is ready to become the wife of "the darkie, as people called him." But Miss Frost's influence is too strong, forcing postponement of the inevitable:

> In her periods of lucidity, when she saw as clear as daylight . . . , she certainly did not love the little man. She felt him a terrible outsider, an inferior, to tell the truth. . . .
> And then, most irritating, a complete *volte face* in her feelings. The clear-as-daylight mood disappeared as daylight is bound to disappear. She found herself in a night where the little man loomed large, terribly large, potent and magical, while Miss Frost had dwindled to nothingness. At such times she wished with all her force that she could travel like a cablegram to Australia. . . . She felt the dark, passionate receptivity of Alexander overwhelmed her, enveloped her even from the Antipodes. She felt herself going distracted—she felt she was going out of her mind. For she could not act.   (pp. 24-25)

Although the engagement is broken off, this episode prefigures fate. Alvina comes in time to choose "night" over the "clear-as-daylight mood," the "inferior," antipodal

figure of Cicio over a conventional lover. Graham's equiva-
lence to Cicio is emphasized when, near the end of the
novel, Alvina finally decides to return to the latter after a
dream of missed opportunities with her first fiancé.

Apart from the episode of the broken engagement, there
are a series of brief incidents in the first third of the novel
designed to bring out in different contexts the contrast of
above and below which is central to the thematic design.
In each case what lies beneath the surface is exposed as more
valuable than that which lies above. By far the richest of
these is the extended description (pp. 47-49) of Alvina's
visionary experience during and immediately after her
visit to the coal mine operated by her father.

Alvina's vision begins by expressing an urgency mainly
relevant to her own position in life but ends by expressing
a larger urgency of vision which is Lawrence's own. This
fantastic passage proceeds by a series of metaphorical leaps
from a prosaic occasion toward an infernal apocalypse out
of which emerges a Laurentian anti-Christ to rule an up-
side-down world. We begin with a girl in a second-rate coal
mine and witness her temporary loss of "lucid" self-aware-
ness as she feels herself in the presence of unknowable
knowledge and melts batlike into fluid darkness. The succeeding vision of the upper world as a glossy scum floating
on a "bubbling up of under-darkness" involves the transformation of the mine into a mythical kingdom of the underworld which is a vassal state under a "superimposed and
tyrannical day-order." Miners become slaves who, it is pre-
dicted, will rise in revolt unless a "dark master" appears in
the upper world to rule. At the end we hear of Alvina's
craving for a debacle in which, presumably, the upper
world, standing for civilization and culture, will be shattered by tremors from beneath.

The framework of *The Lost Girl* is too slight, the pre-

vailing narrative tone too mundane to contain this extraordinary passage of visionary writing. Its motif is eruption and
it erupts volcanically, pouring hot, black lava over the surrounding pages. Nevertheless, it stands out as a central analogy to the imaginative movement that the entire narrative
attempts to work through more prosaically. If we insist on
approaching the description in the wrong spirit seeking to
define its political and social implications the results will
be appalling. But Lawrence's intention here is neither to
predict nor to prophesy. His intention seems to be to project
with maximum poetic intensity and from the point of view
of a devil's advocate his sense of the desolating antinomy
between nature and culture which blights personal and social life everywhere.

Two other rehearsals of the theme of above and below
in this part of the novel transpose the antinomy into less
appalling terms. In the episode of Arthur Witham's accident in the organ loft, the effect is comic-pathetic. Alvina,
starved for a man, contributes her handkerchief as a band-
age for Arthur's hurt leg and then enjoys a swoon "into
oblivion" when he presses her hand down over the wound
for several silent minutes. His action is instinctive and establishes a brief, mindless communion between them which
is broken off when the pain lessens. Witham returns immediately to his unpleasantly conventional manner, leaving
Alvina to reflect sorrowfully over the difference between
the stiff, insentience of a man's clothing and the "vulnerable, hairy, and somehow childish leg of the real man."

A grotesque version of the same contrast is supplied by
the description of the tattooed Japanese vaudeville actor.
When dressed he appears to Alvina as a "shabby-looking
bit of riff-raff of the East," but when he is stripped almost
naked for his appearance on stage Alvina wishes "she
could jump across the space" which separates them. She is

fascinated by the eagle on his back, and by the blue serpent coiling about his thighs and buttocks. Dressed, he exudes an air of toadlike lewdness; naked, he is—to her eye— beautiful.

Each of these foreshadowings constitutes a variation on a common theme. They help render concrete the condition of underneathness and undermine the reader's easy assumption that the actions performed in the daytime world by tightly waistcoated citizens are more real or more important than the impulses lurking in the sentient flesh beneath. As Lawrence rings the changes on this theme the reader's response may vary from amusement to sympathy to shock or to repulsion. Alvina has charm, a certain wistful appeal, and a dogged sort of courage. She is also very much the sex-starved old maid with impulses scandalously ready to break through her self-restraint. Her readiness to leap into the arms of the tattooed man absolutely disqualifies her from the role of romantic heroine. But this, of course, is intentional. Lawrence is interested in clarifying the real relations of instinct and impulse to expressed behavior in an actual environment. Far from romanticizing these human resources he shows their oddness and their deformation under the pressure of societal suppression as well as their power to break through and create for at least one person an entirely new climate of experience.

CICIO AS SYMBOL

The several prefigurations I have discussed are a prologue to the principal narrative episode of *The Lost Girl*— the account of Alvina's struggle to escape the ethical rigors and social satisfactions of the higher self and to enter upon a mindless, purely sensual relationship with Francesco Marasca, called Cicio, a penniless young Italian who possesses what the narrator calls "the sensual secrets" and little

else besides. Life with Cicio means social degradation, loss
of caste, even an admission from Alvina that the communal
judgment on her actions is justified:

> She felt it must be evil. Evil! She was evil. And yet she
> had no power to be otherwise. They were legally married.
> And she was glad.   (p. 298)

Furthermore, it means the acceptance of a position of absolute inferiority to a man who is only aware of her as a
sexual partner, a man barely capable of using language,
who prefers gestures to speech, whose sexual behavior is
by ordinary standards brutally unsympathetic.

If one studies the figure of the young Italian with a view
to puzzling out the meaning of his "sensual secrets," he
will encounter many picturesque descriptions but will reach
no final enlightenment. Cicio is consistently presented in
a double perspective, corresponding with the heroine's am-
bivalent responses to the challenge he offers her. On the
one hand, he is common: he has no manners, his clothes
are in bad taste, he often wears a sneering smile, he is
surly, stupid, loutish; he is out of place in a drawing room,
out of place in a vaudeville troupe, out of place in England.
On the other hand, his dark body seethes with animal grace,
his yellow eyes are leonine, his cleanly modeled features
seem "refined through ages of forgotten culture." Depending on how Alvina is feeling at particular times, his unvary-
ing disharmony with the environment signifies social inferiority or natural superiority. Often she is caught on the
horns of a dilemma, making both responses at once:

> She had a moment of sheer panic. Was he just stupid and
> bestial? The thought went clean through her. His yellow
> eyes watched her sardonically. It was the clean modelling
> of his dark, other-world face that decided her—for it sent
> the deep spasm across her.   (p. 185)

Alvina lingers in this dilemma for nearly two hundred pages. Even after she has married him she goes on raising high-minded questions about what it is precisely that she has done. Why does it take her so long to make the fated choice? To answer the question superficially we might point to Alvina's and Cicio's situations at the time they first meet each other. Alvina is well along in a spinster's career. She accepts the responsibility of looking after her father, pines after a better life, but is mired in dutifulness. Cicio, also, is not free. Along with three other young men from the Continent, he acquiesces sullenly in a strange bondage to the matriarchal Madame Rochard. In order to come together, the lovers must sever old ties. In order to stay together, they must go off to a new place beyond Woodhouse, the Natcha-Kee-Tawara troupe, and England.

Still, given the premise of Alvina's necessary fate, this answer seems incomplete. I would suggest that the long delay is bound up with a central problem which Lawrence faced in *The Lost Girl* of making good an unprecedented artistic intention. He wanted to show in the heroine's career and in terms of the pervasive metaphor of descent, a complete shift of human awareness from a grimly ordinary mode to a much less definable and by no means ordinary mode. Finding few terms available in the tradition of English fiction with which to define the latter kind of awareness he was forced to construct his story as a long set of picturesque variations on a theme. The reader needs time, not so much to look at Cicio, as to listen to the siren song of the narrator's suggestive descriptions if he is to sink at last into an intuition of the powers stirring within the vulgar young Italian. This narrator says in effect: "Yes, he is common, but look again. Perhaps you have been taking commonness too much for granted. Yes, his seduction of

Alvina seems cruel, but she is exchanging an old self for a new one. The pangs she feels are a new parturition."

Thus for example, Cicio's near-rape of the virginal Alvina is imaged in largely negative terms. He suffocates her, kills her, his arms are "horrible." His passion benumbs her like a poisonous drug. It is a very important part of Lawrence's intention to introduce these negative evaluations into the story and then to go on at leisure to teach the reader to see them transvaluated. Alvina's poisoned condition is nasty enough, conventionally regarded. But in the visionary context venom becomes ambrosia, slavery is freedom, suffocation under a cruelly impersonal weight of sexual passion is a new, fresh breath of air. The primary equation is, of course, that down equals up. Alvina falls to rise anew, dies to live, reminding us of the phoenix which Lawrence took as his personal symbol.

The novel's account of the coming together of Alvina and Cicio is, then, a series of variations on a theme quite unexpressible by analytical means. As narrative it has some of the qualities of ballet or modern dance. Expressive gestures, poses, and figural groupings are used to express the ineffable. This can be illustrated by tracing through the novel a series of meetings between Alvina and Cicio which express visually the thematic contrast of above and below and present Alvina's gradual change of heart through changes in the physical position from which she looks at Cicio.

Early in their halting courtship Cicio is nearly always described as crouching, sitting, drooping, or leaning, while Alvina looks down at him from above. The first overt sign of an altered relationship comes when Alvina, in order to coax him back to Madame Rochard's troupe after his flight to Knarborough, enters his room where he is sitting on a bed and stoops down to kiss his hand. A few pages later,

Cicio has returned to his crouch, and Alvina looks down upon him as he squats beside his bicycle, "like a quick-eared animal." The climactic scene comes when Cicio for the first time displays sexual initiative (pp. 180-181). At first Alvina stands on the steps of her house while Cicio looks up at her from the yard, and they watch each other across "a wide, abstract distance." Then Cicio beckons almost imperceptibly with his head while "a dark flicker of ascendency" plays in his eyes. The heroine feels as though her soul has sunk "away out of her body" and comes down to embrace her lover at ground level. As they embrace she looks up at him "like a victim," and he stretches forward over her. After he departs Alvina runs to her bedroom, kneels down, bows her head, experiences physical and emotional sensations which read like a description of birth pangs, then remains crouched over on the floor for some time.

Shortly after this scene Lawrence varies his pattern by permitting the hostile and disparaging Madame Rochard to make explicit comments to Alvina on the subject of Cicio's "underneathness":

> But I know something of these Italian men, who are laborers in every country, just laborers and under-men always, always down, down, down. . . . He will want to rise by you, and you will go down, with him.   (p. 186)

This sounds like a *Daily Express* leader warning Britannia to stop flirting with the Common Market, but what Madame Rochard has to say is true in part. At least for a time Cicio is as attracted by Alvina's prospects of a small inheritance as he is by her person. However, the reader is expected to see a further truth behind Madame's half-truth; that is, social degradation is salvation in the flesh, whereas for Alvina maintenance of social decorum means a fate like her mother's. A few pages later Madame Rochard remarks of Cicio's surname, Marasca, that it has a bad sound: "It sends life down instead of lifting it up." Alvina's rejoinder —"Why should life always go up?"—is what the novel is all about.

After she becomes Cicio's mistress she revaluates his commonness and identifies herself with it. It becomes the triumphant symbol of his and her detachment from the moribund world of industrial England. Riding beside Cicio on the top of a bus one day, Alvina

> was reminded of the woman with the negro husband, down in Lumley. She understood the woman's reserve. She herself felt, in the same way, something of an outcast, because of the man at her side. An outcast! And glad to be an outcast. She clung to Cicio's dark, despised foreign nature. She loved it, she worshipped it, she defied all the other world. Dark, he sat beside her, drawn in to himself, overcast by his presumed inferiority among these northern industrial people. And she was with him, on his side, outside the pale [sic] of her own people.   (p. 222)

However, the love affair does not run very smoothly, and Alvina more than once recoils from her new situation with the reflection that she has "come down in the world, conforming to such standards of life." When she finally runs away from her lover and resumes her old occupation of nursing, she enjoys a sense of improved social position and has no desire to demean herself once again.

The amusing and elaborately staged scene (pp. 284-293) at the house of Mrs. Tukes completes the pattern I have been following. Alvina is nursing the young expectant mother when Cicio appears beneath the windows and begins to sing a shoddy Neapolitan love song. Both women go to the window and peer down into the dark yard from which the song is wafted. Then at Mrs. Tukes's request

Alvina descends reluctantly to give Cicio a rose. Cicio picks up his former mistress and starts to carry her down the road toward Italy, but Mrs. Tukes's labor pains begin—the implication is strong that the animal yearning in his serenade has had something to do with this—and Alvina insists upon returning to the house; but only after she has agreed to go with Cicio to Italy. During Mrs. Tukes's delivery the two women argue the value of intelligence *versus* life. Mrs. Tukes, who is increasingly anti-life as the frequency and intensity of her birth pangs increase, says: "I hate life. It's nothing but a mass of forces. I am intelligent. Life isn't intelligent"; and somehow the figure of Cicio becomes vaguely identified with the Life Force itself. Alvina, whose own struggle to rise in the world is over, advises Mrs. Tukes to submit: "Life is bigger than intelligence."

With Alvina's submission Caliban at last has his way with Miranda; a slight crack opens in the grim façade of the industrial establishment through which an old maid with low tastes in men and an ignorant Italian youth can creep. At best a limited victory, it will seem desperately limited when we look at what becomes of the lovers in Italy. Yet it is a victory, not over intelligence but over a particularly stupid delusion of some civilized people—the delusion that human intelligence has any value when it is cut off from the life of the body and the life of physical feeling. Or—to return to Lawrence's image of the coin—when the head is cut off from the tail.

ITALY AS SYMBOL

Italy as the symbolic place of "sensual" fulfillment remains the last hope of that romantic sort of reader who feels that the earlier chapters have not established beyond the shadow of doubt the full meaning of Cicio's sensual secrets and dark powers. Granted that Cicio cannot show to advantage against the drab background of the industrial Midlands and against the drabber background of theatrical rooming houses and theatres like Houghton's Pleasure Palace, this reader looks to the young hero's Italian homestead in the Abruzzi as a place where his shifty and sullen manner will disappear, where he will stand forth as a splendid archaic figure of atavistic virtues, where he will be able to show us all some rich and vital mysteries.

This does not happen. After the antepenultimate chapter called "The Journey Across," with its vivid evocation of the long journey from England to Califano near Naples during the first weeks of the world war, the final chapters describing Alvina's new life open on a dismal note which is sustained to the end. The narrator not only begins by coolly remarking that Alvina *is* a lost girl but goes on to dwell upon Cicio's utter hopelessness. Natives and Englishwoman alike are in danger of "annihilation" from "the mysterious influence of the mountains and valleys":

> Cicio and Pancrazio clung to her, essentially, as if she saved them also from extinction. Truly, she had to support the souls of the two men.   (p. 324)

The valley is lovely enough, but it is cold, and the farmhouse in which the couple take up residence is bleak and dirty. A ragged peasantry who dwell in the neighborhood distinguish themselves less by their savage grace than by the savagery of their hostile gossip about the wedded pair. Alvina lives from day to day oppressed by a sense of "the awful comfortless meaninglessness of it all." The sexual passion she feels for Cicio continues unabated but fails to rouse him from his settled gloom. At times Alvina is seized by a fierce happiness which is "beyond despair, but very like despair," yet Cicio's despair is unqualified.

These last chapters constitute the breaking of a spell rather than the simple romantic fulfillment of Alvina's dark self. Cicio's magical qualities, so picturesquely evident in England, dissolve here like a mist. The hero emerges as a confused, unhappy, and ignorant young man, miserable over the prospect of being drafted for war service. Alvina, by way of contrast, emerges from benumbed submissiveness, braces her backbone, and replies to Cicio's "I haven't any hope" by snapping, "You have *hope*. Don't make a scene." As the book ends she is, almost literally, holding her young husband up, very much the young Englishwoman of strong character, no longer playing Persephone to Cicio's Hades. The novel ends with a question which remains unanswered and has to do with Cicio's promise to return to Alvina and their unborn child after the war. Whether he will or not remains undetermined; but the reader is free to speculate that if this new, strong-minded, high-minded Alvina has anything to do with it, he will get back.

The final strength and honesty of *The Lost Girl* when compared to a novel like *The Plumed Serpent* lie just in Lawrence's willingness to permit Italy to become actual, to permit the real world to break in upon a visionary and symbolic drama of salvation in the flesh. As long as Cicio was in England, then Italy loomed as that strange land beyond drab reality where masterful men moved gracefully in darkness. It stood for that "dusky region where men had dark faces and translucent yellow eyes, where all speech was foreign, . . . where meanings were all changed." In fact, Italy proves to be no more than another part of Europe; and Califano, apart from its oppressive natural beauty, another Woodhouse without certain civilized conveniences. With that change Alvina's "extraordinary" fate becomes poignantly ordinary. "Darkness" remains but no longer as a glamorous symbol of transformation. At the end it simply and movingly designates the wholly private bond of affection connecting two lovers who face an indefinite separation from each other in a world torn by war.

3

Lady Chatterley's Lover dramatizes two opposed orientations toward life, two distinct modes of human awareness: the one abstract, cerebral, and unvital; the other concrete, physical, and organic. A relatively clear statement of the distinction may be found in Lawrence's long essay, *Apropos of Lady Chatterley's Lover*, written two years after he had published the Florence edition of his novel:

> There are many ways of knowing, there are many sorts of knowledge. But the two ways of knowing, for man, are knowing in terms of apartness, which is mental, rational, scientific, and knowing in terms of togetherness, which is religious and poetic. . . .
> But relationship is threefold. First, there is the relation to the living universe. Then comes the relation of man to woman. Then comes the relation of man to man. And each is a blood-relationship, not mere spirit or mind. We have abstracted the universe into Matter and Force, we have abstracted men and women into separate personalities—personalities being isolated units, incapable of togetherness—so that all three great relationships are bodiless, dead.[3]

The novel's structural method involves a simple juxtaposition of the two modes; its narrative method combines explicit interpretative comment by a narrator who from the beginning makes clear his sympathy for the vitalist

[3] (London: Martin Secker, 1931), pp. 88-89.

viewpoint together with lucid and objective renderings of characters, situations, and settings. Furthermore, there is a sort of synechdochic method employed in the narration. Wragby Hall and the industrial village of Tevershall are realized in themselves but come also to stand for entire industrial, social, and even spiritual orders dominant in the modern world, more especially in twentieth-century England. Sir Clifford Chatterley sums up a modern habit of mind as well as a ruling class in transition from one type of economic proprietorship to another. In contrast, the gamekeeper, Oliver Mellors, not only follows but represents the organic way of life, and the wood in which he lurks is a spatial metaphor of the natural order, or, what Lawrence frequently called "the living universe."

These are but a few of the simple and necessarily rigid equations the novel sets up between particular and general conditions. Of course very few novels have been written which fully resist the regular habit of readers to discover general truths mirrored in particularized and historically limited episodes. But few novels are so explicit and so demanding in the control they impose on the reader's moral imagination as *Lady Chatterley's Lover*.

Among the leading characters only the heroine, Connie Chatterley, plays no rigid representative role; and it is her freedom of action which creates the possibility of drama. As she shuttles from one realm to another—both in space and in terms of inner awareness—from Wragby Hall to the gamekeeper's hut in the woods, her experiences project the energies of the two modes in conflict with one another. She is both booty and battleground in the ensuing struggle between vital and unvital ways of apprehending experience. If it is not too scandalous a suggestion, Lady Chatterley may be said to stand for ourselves, for all those puzzled modern people who have not yet resolved the question of whether they wish to be domiciled at Wragby Hall or in Wragby wood, of whether to live among powerful abstractions or growing things. If the alternatives appear rigidly posed, then that is a limitation which the novel fully accepts. Life can be mapped according to other patterns as even Lawrence knew. But in this story the idea emerges clearly that Lady Chatterley—we—cannot have it both ways. There is no possibility of compromise between vitality and its opposite.[4]

Although the heroine possesses a freedom of role and action unknown to such representative figures as the lord and the gamekeeper, this does not mean that dramatic interest ever depends upon suspense of outcome. From the

[4] In Lawrence's first version of the novel, published fourteen years after his death under the title of *The First Lady Chatterley* (New York: Dial, 1944), Connie indulges in the fantasy of keeping two husbands and does not give up this vain hope until fairly late in the story. She wants to love Clifford's brainy head and simultaneously Parkin's beautiful torso. However, when Lawrence reworked Oliver Parkin into Oliver Mellors for the final version he gave the latter a perfectly good head of his own and strengthened the impression of depravity that Sir Clifford makes. Parkin is a short, homely man, ill-educated and emotionally identified with the working class. Mellors is a tall, slender, well-favored man who looks like a gentleman when dressed up, has been an army officer, reads books, and has severed his ties of loyalty to his proletarian background. At the end of the first version Parkin has decided to remain a Communist and intends to work to infect the working classes with his sexual vitality, so that out of the impending collapse of the social order will survive a few vital men and women able to achieve a way of life based upon "togetherness." At the end of the final version Mellors writes a letter to Connie in which he makes suggestions for the revitalization of English working people, and like Parkin he seems convinced that the present social order is doomed. But he obviously does not intend to proselytize among the workers. The first version, then, has a quasi-political theme—"working classes are depraved but salvageable, managerial and intellectual classes cannot be vitally regenerated"—which fuses with the sexual theme. About the final version no such statement can be made. The expressed attitude is nearer to "a plague on both your houses."

beginning Connie is no more free to choose the realm of "death-in-life" than Alvina Houghton in *The Lost Girl* was free to continue living alone beside her father's shop in Woodhouse. Freedom in the novel is merely relative. In Lawrence's last novel it extends only to questions of means. The heroine must escape her husband and what he stands for; but for a time she is free to entertain various alternatives: to hesitate, to become confused, to relapse, but never finally to make the great refusal.

This is all very much like *The Lost Girl*, but for various reasons much better than that novel. For one thing the later book brings fully into the light ideas and values which in *The Lost Girl* were distorted by equivocal descriptions. In *Lady Chatterley's Lover* only things mysterious in themselves—for example, the sensations of a woman during an orgasm—are described mysteriously. The novel is explicit to the point of pedantry about matters which *The Lost Girl* only managed to treat by indirection. Whereas Cicio possessed "the sensual secrets," Mellors possesses a highly specific sexual technique, a lengthily reported sexual biography, and a prophetic program for his contemporaries which he has worked out in occasionally bizarre detail. If some of Mellors' self-revelations seem absurd, his willingness to take a firm stand on issues crucial to the novel's meaning seems all to the good.

There are other reasons why *Lady Chatterley's Lover* is a much better novel than *The Lost Girl*. First, the realm of the vital is not created as a terminus toward which the heroine moves instinctively, following without thought various obscure hints and signs. Instead it is richly embodied early in the novel and sustained as a genuine meaning to the end. The reader is given the fullest opportunity to appraise the significance of the vital career as it not only is defined through the explicit comments of the narrator and by leading characters like Connie, Mellors, and Dukes, but also realized in imaginative terms of description and dramatization. The heroine is not raped into fulfillment but must use her head as well as her body to escape unwholesome circumstances.

Secondly, the unvital mode is boldly and subtly defined. Woodhouse was an obvious metaphor of death-in-life. Lawrence was by no means the first to flog the dead horse of provincial and small-town mores. But Wragby Hall is something else again. It represents domination not only in the sphere of ideas and sensibility but also in the sphere of economics. Clifford's change of vocation from a writer of ultra-modern stories whose essence is nothingness to that of ultra-modern engineer industrialist developing techniques to exploit further the exhausted mineral soils of his region and to increase the alienation of his workmen from wholesome living conditions is hardly a trivial incident in this connection. The manor house rests on a foundation of abstractions the greatest of which is money. In the struggle between the vital and the anti-vital Sir Clifford holds most if not all the cards. The gamekeeper has no following; he is beset on all sides, and even at the end his victory is by no means clear cut.

A third point of superiority over some of Lawrence's earlier novels can be developed from the previous point. Within the limitations of a particular interpretation of history, culture, and humanity *Lady Chatterley's Lover* appraises the human situation realistically. Abstraction looms large, and vital mysteries shine with but a diminished glimmer in the modern world and in this novel. As Mellors writes to his mistress at the end he mentions "the little glow there is between you and me" and remarks, "all the bad times that ever have been, haven't been able to blow the crocus out." The value of vitality is embodied in tender and vulnerable things, while insentience has the sanction of powerful institutions, individuals, and movements. The story has a restrained quality. After reading it we may find the guarantees of extraordinary developments imperfectly realized in such books as *The Rainbow* and *Women in Love* a sort of whistling in the dark. *Lady Chatterley's Lover* opens with these observations:

> Ours is essentially a tragic age, so we refuse to take it tragically. The cataclysm has happened, we are among the ruins, we start to build up new little habitats, to have new little hopes. It is rather hard work: there is now no smooth road into the future.   (p. 12)

In the context of the whole novel tragedy refers to a great deal more than a world war. The ruins include the abstracted spirit of the age itself. The new habitats and hopes are fixed in such images as that of a little clearing in the midst of a remnant of forest, and in the scrupulously designed description of a man working with his hands to repair a broken pheasant coop. The incommensurability of the little hope and the enormous negation which is modern life is assumed in the novel and does not, I believe, ever become the object of pathetic reflection. After yielding ourselves to the viewpoint dramatized, and after reflecting upon what the last thirty years have contributed to the realization of Lawrence's hopes for the future, we might indeed weep—except that the novel teaches us that the power in life which sustains the crocus is, strictly speaking, unconquerable. Or have we finally reached an intensity of negation where this is no longer true?

A final reason for the superiority of *Lady Chatterley's Lover* is the rich simplicity of its structural design. This design is realized most powerfully and significantly in spatial terms, in terms of setting. The most enduring meanings the novel projects are inextricably bound up with the arrangement of three locations—the manor house, the industrial village, the wood—and their spatial relations with one another under a fume-laden atmosphere which seems to be no better and no worse than Pittsburgh's or northern New Jersey's. Many of Lawrence's novels are built around a central contrast: in *The Rainbow* the contrast is between things as they are and a promised transformation of being; in *The Plumed Serpent* it is between a Europeanized and an aboriginal Mexico; in *The Lost Girl* it is between "higher" and "lower" selves, or, spatially, between Woodhouse and southern Italy. All these contrasts from one point of view come to the same thing. They express the opposition between "two ways of knowing."

In *Lady Chatterley's Lover* the same contrast is represented through settings which impinge on one another, which coexist at the same time, in the same district. There is no appeal to the strange and far to fix either side of the contrast and no direct appeal to the future. The novel concentrates its drama within the space of a few square miles, and Lawrence summons all his powers of description to present this space as it is: a portion of English soil in transition from a semi-rural, semi-industrial condition to one of total industrialization. If the novel demands that we regard these few miles as an epitome of the larger world of Western Civilization itself, we may find it easy to assent because in so many ways Lawrence's microcosm looks and smells like the world we know.

The wood is the vital center of Lawrence's panorama. It is menaced on one side by the ugly houses and mining installations of the colliery village; on the other it is owned but not valued by the occupants of the dreary manor house. There is social and economic hostility between village and manor, but both workers and owner unite in opposition to everything the wood represents. Both worship the abstractions of money, power, and property, and both are devoted to the mechanistic organization of human affairs. The wood stands approximately in between two forces of negation. It is Lawrence's sacred wood within which life-mysteries are enacted. These are of birth, budding, and growth, embodied in the annual cycle of fertility in tree, flower, and animal, humanly embodied also in the sexual encounters between the gamekeeper and the lady; for out of these encounters proceed a rebirth of feeling in both people, the possibility of a new life together, and finally the promise of a child. The love affair moves in phase with the organic burgeoning of the wood during a wet but beautiful spring. It extends from the time of the first flowers to a time when the trees and flowers are in full bloom.

The religious or mythic aspect of the woodland setting is most fully realized in a lovely passage from the first version of the novel which Lawrence did not carry forward into the final version. It occurs after Connie has had her first sexual experience with Parkin:

> She was filled, herself, with an unspeakable pleasure, a pleasure which has no contact with speech. She felt herself filled with new blood, as if the blood of the man had swept into her veins like a strong, fresh, rousing wind, changing her whole self. All her self felt alive, and in motion, like the woods in spring. She could not but feel that a new breath had swept into her body from the man, and that she was like a forest soughing with a new, soft wind, soughing and moving unspoken into bud. All her body felt like the dark interlacing of the boughs of an oak wood, softly humming in a wind, and humming inaudibly with the myriad, myriad unfolding of buds. Meanwhile the birds had their heads laid on their shoulders and slept with delight in the vast interlaced intricacy of the forest of her body.
>
> From the man, from the body of the man, the pure wind had swept in on her. . . .

And meanwhile the voice of the other man, Sir Clifford, went on and on, clapping and gurgling with strange sound. Not for one second did she really hear what he said. But it sounded to her like the uncouth cries and howls of barbarous, disconnected savages dancing around a fire somewhere outside the wood. Clifford was a smeared and painted savage howling in an utterly unintelligible gibberish somewhere on the outskirts of her consciousness. She, deep within the sacred and sensitive wood, was filled with the pure communication of the other man, a communication delicate as the inspiration of the gods.   (pp. 52-53)

Here the woman's consciousness becomes fused through metaphor with the wood itself, so that she can carry its mystery indoors with her. Lawrence uses the traditional religious image of the wind to express how she has become inspired. Notice, also, the inversion whereby the civilized becomes the savage—Clifford has been reading aloud from Racine!—whereas the sensations of well-being after an erotic experience are defined in pentecostal terms.

For no character in the novel is the wood a natural and inevitable habitat. Connie and Mellors are both somewhat battered products of unwholesome civilization who, as it were, stumble onto sacred ground while following paths leading from opposite sides. Mellors arrives first from the direction of Tevershall; the lady comes trailing down some months later from the "eminence" on which Wragby sits. In the not wholly adequate shelter of a remnant of Sherwood Forest they create through the sex act that condition of interconnection which is the *sine qua non* of escape from the "tragic" world but which certainly does not guarantee that escape.

The wood symbolizes not only a way of life but also the beleaguered and vulnerable status to which the vital career has been reduced. The vastness of the original forest has declined under the steady attrition of civilization to a thin wood which barely conceals the lovers from prying eyes and barely provides cover for the pheasants and rabbits which are its only wildlife. Mellors grimly tracks down the colliers who poach on his preserves, but there are other kinds of invasion that he is powerless to resist. From Tevershall comes the obscene Bertha Couts to fill the sensitive glade with domestic uproar, and from Wragby comes Clifford in his motorized chair to ride down the wild flowers while musing on the felicities and responsibilities of being a property owner. For reasons of family pride the Chatterleys have been interested in preserving the remaining forest. But we are told that this interest can yield to "higher" claims. During the late war, Clifford's father, Sir Geoffrey, in an excess of patriotic zeal had cut hundreds of trees to provide trench timber for the troops in Belgium and France:

> On the crown of the knoll where the oaks had stood, now was bareness; and from there you could look out over the trees to the colliery railway, and the new works at Stacks Gate. Connie had stood and had looked, it was a breach in the pure seclusion of the wood. It let in the world.   (p. 47)

Throughout the novel we are made aware of this process of attrition, as if in a short time the trees and glades will disappear, leaving village and hall locked—like the aristocratic Sir Clifford and the plebeian Mrs. Bolton at the end of the story—in monstrous, unvital embrace. Finally, not only is the wood surrounded, but also it is being attacked from beneath. The vertical shafts of the local mines lead to horizontal corridors fanning out in all directions. The rich soil of Wragby Wood is undermined by coal diggings, while its flora and fauna are being reduced at ground level. Simultaneously from the skies come poisonous fumes and "smuts" to sicken the vegetation and reduce the vigor of the animals. All in all it is through his power to project a crisis of industrial civilization in these concrete terms that Lawrence is able to make his point compelling.

Since the central theme of *Lady Chatterley's Lover* is concreteness *versus* abstraction, it is appropriate that the success of Lawrence's representative method should depend largely on richly concrete realizations of persons, settings, and situations, that the power of his prophecy should depend on the power of his art to particularize meanings which suggest broader conditions and widely applicable truths of experience. Here I want to examine some features of the two opposed modes or realms of experience as they are fictionally embodied and to raise some questions both about the artistic success of these representations and about the ideas to which they may be referred. Although the story proceeds in a dialectical movement, usually alternating scenes at Wragby with scenes in the gamekeeper's domain, there is no reason why we cannot examine each realm in turn.

DEATH-IN-LIFE

An abiding impression of Sir Clifford and of most of the intellectuals who foregather at Wragby Hall during the early part of the story is that they are not very real. But this hardly supplies a ground for criticism of the portrayal of Sir Clifford since his unreality is precisely the point the novel makes. He is a "hurt thing," a "lost thing" whose capacity to be involved in life has been destroyed by the war. He is able to think and to experience egoistic feeling but cannot get in touch. It seems to his wife, and nothing happens in the story to contradict her view, that at the core of him there is only "a negation of human contact." His is not a problem of war neurosis or of the psychology of invalidism. Perhaps the best way to regard him is in the nature of an experimental hypothesis: given such and such conditions, then what other conditions will result? Looked at in this way, the character remains interesting throughout the novel and vibrates with a queer mechanical energy, like those incredibly energetic yet two-dimensional characters one finds in Dickens and in the novels of Smollett and Fielding.

The hypothesis may be stated as follows: what will a man do with himself and with others when his physical attachment to experience has been violently and traumatically severed? The novel's answer is that such a man will create a "simulacrum of reality," a complex pattern of abstract relationships to substitute for felt connections between himself and others. Within this pattern or web he will enjoy the illusion of life, but all the time he will not be alive at all. Here one might remark that the "adjustment" is harmless enough, but this ignores the problem of others. Actually, Clifford's first great crime is that he draws his wife into his orbit of nonexistence. The abstracted man who cannot live in himself leans with crushing weight on his partner. He slowly draws from her those vital energies which sustain her in being, but can only waste what he absorbs since nothing can restore him to life.

In this depiction of Clifford's parasitism Lawrence is working once again with an assumption which is basic to all his work. It is that there is life in the vital sense and death in the sense of the unvital but no third thing, no possibility of an attitude of nonattachment—one which neither preys on the vitality of others nor is based on the capacity of physical self-realization. In Lawrence generally the ground of all value is physical experience. This is both his characteristic limitation and the theme that unifies all his works—

fiction, poetry, essays, and treatises. The only reality and the only marvel is to be alive in the flesh. At the same time an individual can experience his aliveness only through direct relationship with another living thing. He can fuse himself in contemplation with the life of trees, flowers, or animals, but the crucial experience of relatedness is, appropriately enough, a sexual experience with a woman: appropriate because it conforms to the order of nature, because for Lawrence touch is a more powerful mode of connectedness than sight, because sex is, in sensory and emotional terms, a stronger experience of connection than any other.

All this can be put into a single doctrinal statement: to know and possess oneself is to have experienced a unity with live things and persons outside oneself. These Laurentian convictions are primarily a product of intuition, but they receive some reinforcement in the speculations of at least one major modern philosopher. A. N. Whitehead has presented similar conclusions about men's relations to a "living universe" in his essay "Nature Alive,"[5] although needless to say he does not concern himself with the sexual relation. But Whitehead argues that all mental experience is derived from bodily functioning and that strictly speaking no one can determine where our bodies end and where the surrounding physical environment begins. A man is alive in nature and nature is alive in him; his sense of self is included in his sense of otherness, and *vice versa*. Therefore, "togetherness" is not only a way of knowing but the fundamental mode of being.

Clifford's first pattern of abstraction is created with words. As a writer he spins verbal cobwebs, and in his daily association with Connie he invariably tries to reduce concrete experience to formulae. He attempts to fill the void

[5] The essay is contained in *Modes of Thought* (New York: Macmillan, 1938).

between his wife and himself with phrases like "the habit of intimacy," and "our steadily-lived life." But within his orbit the only reality for Connie is "nothingness, and over it a hypocrisy of words." Because he accepts words as a facsimile of reality, verbal connections as a substitute for felt connections, he comes to worship success. He wishes to be talked about, written about, recognized as something, because he is nothing. And, although wealthy and not avaricious, he seeks money as the visible yet abstract emblem of success.[6]

In mid-career Clifford orients himself in a new pattern of abstraction. This time it is economic and industrial power that give him the illusion of life. He is brilliantly successful at developing new methods of mining organization because he sees human beings only as functions of an abstractly formulated process, not as flesh-and-blood realities. His social views are summed up in his slogan, "the function determines the individual"—a man *is* no more than what he does. Now Clifford is in a position to commit far greater crimes than before. As an industrialist he draws men and women by the thousands into his orbit of nonexistence. He becomes a leader in a civilized society described at one point by the word "insane" and gains new confidence and toughness from his success in manipulating men and machines. He is described as becoming "almost a *creature*, with a hard, efficient shell of an exterior and a pulpy interior, one of the amazing crabs and lobsters of the modern industrial and financial world, invertebrates of the crustacean order, with

[6] In the first version Clifford is very much a Platonist. In the final version this is played down but survives in such scenes as the one in which he is impressed favorably by a certain book whose thesis is that the universe is materially wasting but spiritually ascending. Connie demurs violently, arguing that Plato, Aristotle, and Jesus killed off the human body, and it is "only just coming to real life." For the whole debate see *Lady Chatterley's Lover*, pp. 280-284.

shells of steel, like machines, and inner bodies of soft pulp."
From the pulp of his inner life emanate just two vibrations
—an impulse of self-assertion and a contradictory impulse
of terrified dependency. When Connie casts him off he
transfers this dependency to Mrs. Bolton, and at the end
is left in a strange state of equilibrium:

> After this, Clifford became like a child with Mrs. Bolton.
> He would hold her hand, and rest his head on her breast,
> and when she once lightly kissed him, he said: "Yes! Do
> kiss me! Do kiss me!" And when she sponged his great
> blond body, he would say the same: "Do kiss me!" and
> she would lightly kiss his body, anywhere, half in mockery.
>
> And he lay with a queer, blank face like a child, with a
> bit of the wonderment of a child. And he would gaze on
> her with wide, childish eyes, in a relaxation of madonna-
> worship. . . .
>
> Mrs. Bolton was both thrilled and ashamed, she both
> loved and hated it. Yet she never rebuffed or rebuked him.
> And they drew into a closer physical intimacy, an intimacy
> of perversity, when he was a child stricken with an apparent
> candour and an apparent wonderment, that looked almost
> like a religious exaltation: the perverse and literal rendering
> of "except ye become again as a little child."—While she
> was the Magna Mater, full of power and potency, having the
> great blond child-man under her will and stroke entirely.
>
> The curious thing was that when this child-man, which
> Clifford was now and which he had been becoming for years,
> emerged into the world, it was much sharper and keener
> than the real man he used to be. . . . It was as if his very
> passivity and prostitution to the Magna Mater gave him in-
> sight into material business affairs, and lent him a certain
> remarkable inhuman force. The wallowing in private emo-
> tion, the utter abasement of his manly self, seemed to lend
> him a second nature, cold, almost visionary, business-clever.
> In business he was quite inhuman.   (pp. 352-353)

As a portrait of the modern businessman Clifford is sure-ly no better than a monstrous caricature. It would be incor-rect to regard him as the imaginative representation of some such cliché of popular psychology as "Men who succeed in business are often emotionally underdeveloped and in-fantile." It would be more appropriate to see him as a kind of imagined limit toward which certain tendencies in mod-ern life might be moving. Real men fall somewhere be-tween the limits defined at one extreme by Sir Clifford Chatterley and at the other by the gamekeeper.

The narrative presentation of Clifford is carefully han-dled so as to prevent the reader ever coming at the char-acter directly. His utterances are invariably hedged round with interpretative comment by the narrator or by Connie which draws out the depraved implications of what he says and does. He is always an illustration of disconnectedness; never for a moment does he emerge as a man who has suf-fered a terrible wound and is to be pitied for it. If even briefly the reader could feel with him as a human being, then his whole characterization would seem terribly cruel, and Lawrence's demonstration would be fatally flawed. But the truth is that Clifford in this novel is himself a man en-tirely defined by his functions. There is nothing left over to pity. Riding about the estate in his motorized chair he is a kind of mechanical centaur who, because he is only half hu-man, is not human at all. Voidness cannot be villainous, nor can it become an object of sympathy.

Clifford is essential to the novel, but the same cannot be said for those characters who sit about in the drawing room at Wragby discussing the superiority of mind over matter and revealing their diseased attitudes toward love, working people, and the sex act. Insofar as many of these people—Lady Bennerley, Charles May, Hammond, and Tommy Dukes—are devitalized, two-dimensional creatures,

THE DEED OF LIFE

they are no more than tautological variations on Clifford himself. Their discussions seem hopelessly dated. These characters do not appear in the first version of the novel and add little to the final version. Dukes, of course, is a spokesman for the vital and "phallic" consciousness: "Real knowledge comes out of the whole corpus of the conscious-ness; out of your belly and your penis as much as out of your brain and mind." In saying this he anticipates the views of Mellors, but it is hard to see why such press agen-try should be necessary. When Mellors enters the story, it soon turns out that he can speak for himself, sometimes to the point of tediousness. Dukes in his own words is a "mental-lifer" who holds the right ideas but cannot act upon them. He is the Hamlet, or rather the Prufrock, of *Lady Chatterley's Lover*.

The novel's second powerful representation of "death-in-life" is concentrated in a set passage of description oc-curring about midway in the story. It is a genuine *tour de force* running on for eleven pages and covering in meticu-lous detail the physical appearance of three industrial vil-lages and the many miles of semi-industrial countryside which lie around them. Things seen are richly rendered as fact and simultaneously judged and analyzed by the newly awakened heroine, Connie Chatterley. It is dramatically appropriate that she should interpret her impressions as she does. At the same time the entire description may easily stand as Lawrence's own last indignant comment on the crimes perpetrated by an industrial civilization against es-sential human needs and capacities.

Connie drives from Wragby through Tevershall, the new village of Stacks Gate, and on to Uthwaite, an old Midland village where the Chatterley family are still looked upon as country gentry. In and around the villages she observes coal miners and other workmen, working-class homes and shopping districts, schools, churches, factories, pubs, and hotels. Her perspective is constantly shifting as the car mounts hills and drops down into valleys, crawls through narrow streets crowded with traffic, or runs swiftly through open country. In the end this moving panorama of an entire district creates a striking and large image of human disorder spread out upon a portion of the earth's surface scarred and ravaged by man himself.

To the heroine the hideousness of these raw villages expresses much the same meaning as Wragby and its master. Ugliness is seen as evidence of "the utter absence of the instinct for shapely beauty which every bird and beast has, the utter death of the human intuitive faculty." As she hears school children bawling out a song in one of the new school buildings she asks, "What could possibly become of such people, a people in whom the living intuitive faculty was dead as nails, and only queer mechanical yells and uncanny will-power remained?" These observations are not sentimental, nor are they validated by any program of social or economic reform she has in mind for the improvement of the lives of the industrial masses. Instead the natural grace and vigor of human beings left free to express themselves in physical and instinctive ways is the assumption from which criticism follows. No social or economic class is assigned full blame for producing the "half-corpses" of the "new race of mankind" although there is a vague distinction between leaders and led in the questions "Ah God, what has man done to man? What have the leaders of men been doing to their fellow man?"

Actually, the description embodies a mordant irony. Connie observes that the new mining villages and industrial installations are crowding in upon the parks and manors of the rich, cultivated people of the district. These magnates had set the industrial process in motion when they first began to exploit the mineral resources of their hitherto rural properties. Their desire for profits had created the conditions which produced the dehumanization of the workers and the denaturing of soil and atmosphere. Now the miners, "elemental creatures, weird and distorted, of the mineral world," build their houses at the very gates of the manor parks. The owners are being shoved out of their places by the inhuman pressure of the industrial masses for living room:

> This is history. One England blots out another. The mines had made the halls wealthy. Now they were blotting them out, as they had already blotted out the cottages. The industrial England blots out the agricultural England. One meaning blots out another. . . . And the continuity is not organic, but mechanical.   (p. 186)

The description as a whole does not protest change as such, or rest its case on an imagined superiority of past to present. The real protest is against a change which seems to be altogether uncontrolled by human beings. Men have made a machine—industrial civilization—and now the machine proceeds to make men—in its own image. In the end there can be no distinction between victim and victimizer because the machine, manned by dehumanized creatures like Sir Clifford and the half-corpses whom he employs, victimizes all alike. This pessimistic conclusion is most pointedly expressed by the gamekeeper as he looks out at night from his leafy shelter toward the nearby industrial area:

> The fault lay there, out there, in those evil electric lights and diabolical rattlings of engines. There in the world of the mechanical greedy, greedy mechanism and mechanized greed, sparkling with lights and gushing hot metal and roaring with traffic, there lay the vast evil thing, ready to destroy whatever did not conform. Soon it would destroy the wood,

and the bluebells would spring no more. All vulnerable things must perish under the rolling and running of iron. (p. 140)

The profound sense of crisis communicated by the description I have been discussing depends partly on the patience and skill with which closely observed facts of daily experience have been grouped to make a unified, overwhelming impression, partly on the validity of the idea that underlies the description. The idea is that men, because they are alive, cannot without fatal injury to themselves be subordinated to that which is not alive. Living is not a matter of functions but of the organic wholeness and health of a physical species. Industrialism, insofar as it maims the human organism, or forces it to form a shell of insentience to protect its vulnerable substance, defeats the great human ends for which it was designed. Lawrence's attack on industrialism is not conducted on idealistic grounds. It stems from his keen sense that men and women, like tree, bird, and flower, are physically alive and growing. This is the basic human reality, and all higher possibilities depend upon the healthy condition of the physical man and woman.

Perhaps we are so used to the demands civilization makes upon us to regard our bodies merely as serviceable instruments that we cannot respond to Lawrence's insistence that *our bodies are our selves* and that the only way to be alive is in the flesh. But it seems to me he has discovered the perfect place to rest a case against an industrial civilization. For no one pretends that such a civilization offers spiritual rewards to its supporters. It offers merely the promise of a richer material existence, and Lawrence suggests that the offer is a swindle. What is given by one hand is taken away by the other, since dead men cannot appreciate, except in a simulated way, the benefits of life. On this view all wars are lost, all five-year plans fail, because men cannot wage military battles or battles of production without dying "vitally." This is because vulnerability and tenderness are of the essence of the human, and these qualities cannot be preserved in large, difficult enterprises requiring the subordination of individuals to impersonal processes. A man must live in the now; if he does not, he will find himself dead in the hereafter.

To cope with the argument on its own terms one might grant the tendency of the "insentient iron world" to maim and destroy the vital essence of human beings, but argue that Lawrence overplays vulnerability and tenderness. Is it possible that the "human intuitive faculty," anchored as it is in the powerful surges of the body's life, can survive the ugliness and disintegration of factory towns and the inhuman efficiency of assembly lines? Does it not seem true that toughness alike with sensitiveness is demonstrated in the power of most growing things to maintain themselves in being? Granted that the basis of endurance is the same in man and crocus, is the man less hardy than the crocus? Perhaps the Laurentian answer would be that the crocus knows when it is time to die, but many human beings, who ought to accept the fact that they are already dead, fashion for themselves a simulacrum and continue during some years to spread death among the living in the manner of Clifford Chatterley.

THE VITAL REALM

Constance Chatterley's trip into Wragby Wood is, in the symbolic terms the novel establishes, a journey from death into life and from the profoundly unreal into reality. Wragby is dominated by the word, and, as Lawrence remarks in a passage of *Apropos of Lady Chatterley's Lover*, the word is insufficient to establish that "vivid and nourishing relation to the cosmos and the universe" which is man's only hope of sustaining himself fulfilled in the midst of life:

> It is no use asking for a Word to fulfil such a need. No Word, no Logos, no Utterance will ever do it. The Word is uttered, most of it; we need only pay true attention. But who will call us to the Deed, the great Deed of the Seasons and the year, the Deed of the soul's cycle, the Deed of a woman's life at one with a man's. . . . It is the *Deed* of life we have now to learn: we are supposed to have learnt the Word, but, alas, look at us. Word-perfect we may be, but Deed-demented. Let us prepare now for the death of our present "little" life, and the re-emergence in a bigger life, in touch with the moving cosmos.[7]

This is the prophetic dimension in which the reader must view the heroine's quest. At the same time, it would be foolish to deny that from another perspective Constance Chatterley is merely a bored society woman of rather low moral character who is swept forward into fulfillment in spite of herself. Her personal background, her girlish sexual adventures with German students in the Black Forest, her nerve-wracking affair with the careerist, Michaelis, contain nothing to admire. Her only qualification for the role of heroine is a capacity to come alive in the body, to become awakened instinctually, and to be "at one with a man's life." But of course this is the only qualification demanded. Connie's lack of distinction is all to the good if we agree that her reorientation in life is enacted convincingly since then her success holds out a promise to all. To confer on an ordinary woman an extraordinary fate and to suggest that there is no other fate worth seeking is what *Lady Chatterley's Lover*, like *The Lost Girl* before it, tries to do. The earlier novel is less successful because it presents no clearly described experience embodying the "vivid rela-

[7] *Apropos*, pp. 81-82.

tion," no setting where that relation is convincingly enacted. The sexual episodes in the "sacred" wood are dramatic experience embodying such a relation in *Lady Chatterley's Lover*. Less ambiguously than in any earlier novel
Lawrence completes his main mission here by balancing rejection against affirmation, the attack on an insensate civilization against a celebration of creative possibilities in warm-
ly physical, interpersonal human experience. When the sexual scenes are looked at in this way, the importance of their
function in the total action becomes evident. Union in
sexual experience demands as concrete expression as does
disconnectedness at Wragby and in the industrial environs.

The only serious argument that can be raised against
these scenes has to do with the inadequacy of words—any
words—to set forth the meaning and drama of intimate
physical and emotional experiences in which consciousness,
on the narrator's own admission, surges in a dimension of
reality inaccessible to language. For example let us consider
the following passage from a scene in which Connie and the
gamekeeper come to a sexual climax together:

> And it seemed she was like the sea, nothing but dark
> waves rising and heaving, heaving with a great swell, so
> that slowly her whole darkness was in motion, and she was
> ocean rolling its dark, dumb mass. Oh, and far down inside
> her the deeps parted and rolled asunder, in long, far-travell-
> ing billows, and ever, at the quick of her, the depths parted
> and rolled asunder from the center of soft plunging, as the
> plunger went deeper and deeper, touching lower, and she
> was deeper and deeper and deeper disclosed, and heavier the
> billows of her rolled away to some shore, uncovering her,
> and closer and closer plunged the palpable unknown, and
> further and further rolled the waves of herself away from
> herself, leaving her, till suddenly, in a soft, shuddering
> convulsion the quick of all her plasm was touched . . . and
> she was gone. She was gone, she was not, and she was born:
> a woman.   (p. 208)

This is beautiful enough in its way, but somehow these heavy rhythms and overlapping repetitions of word and phrase seem verbose. The narrator cannot adequately synthesize this sort of experience in words any more than one might adequately describe the circulation of the blood from an "inside" viewpoint. The description has some good features. It avoids the grey vocabulary of sexual science; it is ingenious in its attempt to match up verbal rhythms with the mounting neural tensions of sexual excitation. But ingenuity is hardly enough to do the job here. The reader fails to achieve any deep realization of the sexual mystery and instead is liable to find himself stopping to ask questions about the plain prose meaning of such things as "the quick of the plasm," the statement that this woman has now become a woman (what was she a few moments earlier?), or the statement that at the height of the experience "she was not."

In a piece of music like Wagner's *Liebestod* sequence in *Tristan Und Isolde*, which might be interpreted as orgasmic, such questions do not arise. Given the kind of materials he works with, any composer may conceivably create in a structure of pure sound a perfect analogue of the feminine sexual climax. Words, however, ordinarily cannot do this, unless they are wrenched from normal grammatical relationship and purified of their ordinary signific meanings. Here the narrator does not choose to withdraw from the scene; Lawrence does not choose to develop some version of the stream of consciousness technique which could render the kind of pure suggestiveness music is capable of rendering. The ocean-swimmer: woman-man analogy on which the passage is built remains curiously formal, not quite an argument but too much like an argument to overwhelm and flood the reader's awareness with emotive meanings.

The problem of language is less intense when less central

features of sexual relations are described or dramatized, but it is still there. The gamekeeper's use of the dialect and of the Anglo-Saxon four-letter words possesses the sort of charm that cloys in repetition. Perhaps the slurs, elisions, and crooning sounds of Midlands vernacular are more appropriate to tender, erotic conversations than the tight-lipped accents of Received Standard British, but this is something difficult for an American reader to judge. Also, the four-letter words will or will not have their effect depending on a reader's personal background. They may seem fresh, honest, and direct to someone who has never heard them used eight or ten times to a sentence by ordinary, unvital men in discussions of the news, politics, baseball, and movies. For this reader most of their magic had been rubbed off before he was out of grammar school.

I would suggest that after a certain point the sexual scenes simply are not available for the usual kinds of critical analysis. Most criticism bases itself on the assumption that a community of intelligent readers will make somewhat similar responses to the same material. Criticism seeks to articulate those responses and to discover their ground in the reading material itself. But here, if there is anything in Lawrence's belief that modern civilization corrupts or disorganizes man's sexual nature, it becomes clear that every reader must go his own way, giving his impressions without expecting much support from other readers. Objectivity becomes impossible. My own impression is that some of the renderings of sexual intimacy are beautiful and convincing. More often there is too much solemnity in the speeches and attitudes of both man and woman. Certain scenes seem downright silly: Mellors' address to his penis (p. 252); the scene in which Connie and Mellors wreathe flowers about each other's bodies with particular attention to the pubic zone (pp. 265-276).

It is easier to understand why we should be given so much nakedness and so many descriptions of the sexual experience than to make fine distinctions between degrees of effectiveness in particular scenes. The insentient outer world denies the primary value of the body's physical life and aspires toward an ideal condition of disembodiment. But in the wood, where this value is asserted, naked contact between the physical man and woman is more important than anything else. Furthermore, the closest possible contact comes in sexual intercourse, an experience defined by the novel as a fusion into a temporary unity of man with woman, woman with man, the two together with the secret heart of life. The possibility of a rebirth of wholesome feeling is grounded in the sex act because only at the moment of orgasm does the individual escape his self-obsession into identification with the "living universe." When he or she returns from his blind mystical illumination—one which is not separable from the powerful sensual feelings that momentarily overwhelm ordinary awareness—he discovers himself to be *changed*, as if he had looked into the face of God Himself. This is mysticism. One needs not assume in making use of the term that such experiences are "unreal," only that, like more orthodox varieties of the experience, it will never yield up its meaning to the nonmystic. As Connie Chatterley lies with her lover in a condition described as "one perfect concentric fluid of feeling" she utters inarticulate little cries. The narrator's reverent comment is that here we have "the voice out of the uttermost night, the life!" It is easier to believe in this miracle—a miracle because it is not the woman crying out but the voice of the universe itself—than to comprehend it.

The reader may more easily come to terms with that part of the redemptory pattern of action which leads up to the sexual scenes. The first sexual encounter between gamekeeper and heroine actually completes rather than begins the drama of her passing over from one life-orientation to another. For Connie this process of transition is painful, and it is poignantly realized in some of the most moving descriptive-dramatic passages in the novel. The sexual scenes succeeding the first really add nothing new. Connie has her moments of resistance. She has to undergo a sort of basic training in the arts of the vital career, and later chapters take up the practical problem of how the lovers are to translate their adulterous connection into a permanent living arrangement. But when the heroine first enters the hut to give herself to her husband's servant, she has crossed the gulf between the unliving and the living. The central action is substantially complete.

This action of passing over is presented as a series of definable moments of realization. The process is not wholly internalized or reflective, for each hesitant step forward follows an occasion in which Connie comes into contact with some form of the vital outside herself. The mode of contact is at first visual. Later other modes of perception come into play, and finally it is a touch which gently presses her forward into fulfillment. To conclude my discussion of the "vital realm" I shall trace this process in some detail.

A point of departure is established during a walk in the woods with Sir Clifford. Connie is bored with life, entangled in a shoddy love affair with Michaelis, entangled in the web of Clifford's phrases about the steadily lived life. Suddenly, the new gamekeeper, whom Connie has never met, emerges from a sidepath in the wood "like the sudden rush of a threat out of nowhere":

> She was watching a brown spaniel that had run out of
> a side-path, and was looking towards them with lifted nose,
> making a soft, fluffy bark. A man with a gun strode swiftly,
> softly out after the dog, facing their way as if about to attack

them; then stopped instead, saluted, and was turning down hill. It was only the new game-keeper, but he had frightened Connie, he seemed to emerge with such a swift menace. (p. 52)

The description simultaneously expresses the heroine's alienation from what is real and suggests that, unlike Clifford, she is not beyond cure. Although frightened she is not indifferent. The threat conceals a promise which she is not yet capable of realizing, but when she turns her attention back to Clifford and Wragby, her sense of the profound meaninglessness of her existence has become intensified.

For a time after this encounter Connie makes no progress out of her condition of alienation. As a man the gamekeeper seems to her to be aloof, surly, even hostile. She continues her affair with the writer and goes on accepting "the great nothingness of life" as "the one end of living." She does, however, get into the habit of taking long walks in the woods alone, but it is wintertime and even the trees seem to her to express only "depth within depth of grey, hopeless inertia, silence, nothingness."

Connie is shocked into awareness for the second time when by accident she observes the gamekeeper washing himself in the open air behind his cottage. A commonplace experience becomes "visionary" when for some moments this woman who has devoted her life to nothingness recognizes that she is in the presence of something. Her conscious mind rejects the vision, but "in her womb" she knows she has been exposed to a reality which is fundamental and concrete: "the warm, white flame of a single life, revealing itself in contours that one might touch: a body." When she returns home she strips off her clothing before a mirror and examines her own body inch by inch. Painfully, she recognizes that it is becoming meaningless and ugly. She has been swindled out of her first youth by what she calls "the mental life," with its abstractness and its neglect of the body as an essential human reality.

From here on she is in covert rebellion against her husband's world. At the same time Mellors remains withdrawn and suspicious. She increases the frequency of her walks in the woods during the month of March and experiences a whole series of recognitions which can be turned back as perspectives on her own dynamic state of being. On a cold, brilliant March day she enters the woods while certain phrases sweep through her consciousness:

Ye must be born again! I believe in the resurrection of the body! Except a grain of wheat fall into the earth and die, it shall by no means bring forth. When the crocus cometh forth I too will emerge and see the sun!
(pp. 98-99)

The wind, described as the breath of Persephone, who is "out of hell on a cold morning," and as though it were trying to break itself free of the branches in which it has become entangled, excites her. An identification between the woman and the wind is established through the emphasis on the idea of escape and release. She sits with her back against a young pine tree and becomes excited as it sways against her "elastic and powerful, rising up." The description, of course, has phallic overtones and foreshadows some of the phallic rituals which take place in later sexual scenes. But what makes these descriptions beautiful and exciting for the reader is the imaginative power with which the idea is communicated that there is a real connection between the life springing in the reawakened woods and the changing, revitalized feeling of the woman.

To be at one with the life of the woods is a great deal in itself. Nevertheless the heroine's change of awareness cannot be arrested at this Thoreauvian point of vital realization. She is now "loose and adrift" between the old life and the new, and must exert herself to find new moorings. From this point on it is only the reluctance of the game-keeper to become himself reawakened under the patheti-cally inadequate auspices of the beleaguered wood which de-lays fate. Day after day Connie comes to the little clearing to watch Mellors at work performing the wholesome tasks of pheasant husbandry and then returns home alone to Wragby where Mrs. Bolton has already begun to replace her as Clifford's companion and nurse. The gamekeeper remains wary until the beautiful scene in which Connie takes up a newly born pheasant chick in her hand, then bows herself down and weeps:

Connie crouched in front of the last coop. The three chicks had run in. But still their cheeky heads came poking sharply through the yellow feathers, then withdrawing, then only little beady head eyeing forth from the vast mother-body.

"I'd love to touch them," she said, putting her fingers gingerly through the bars of the coop. But the mother-hen pecked at her hand fiercely, and Connie drew back startled and frightened.

"How she pecks at me! She hates me!" she said in a wondering voice. "But I wouldn't hurt them!"

The man standing above her laughed, and crouched down beside her, knees apart, and put his hand with quiet confidence slowly into the coop. The old hen pecked at him, but not so savagely. And slowly, softly, with sure gentle fingers, he felt among the old bird's feathers and drew out a faintly-peeping chick in his closed hand.

"There!" he said, holding out his hand to her. She took the little drab thing between her hands, and there it stood, on its impossible little stalks of legs, its atom of balancing life trembling through its almost weightless feet into Connie's hands. But it lifted its handsome, clean-shaped little head

> boldly, and looked sharply round, and gave a little "peep."
> "So adorable! So cheeky!" she said softly.
> The keeper, squatting beside her, was also watching
> with an amused face the bold little bird in her hands. Sud-
> denly he saw a tear fall on to her wrist.   (p. 135)

She has been moved by the touch of new life in the tiny
bird who stands so boldly on her outstretched hands. She
weeps because her own maternal instincts have been frus-
trated, because her life is emotionally barren, because she
is a woman without a warm physical connection with anybody or anything. Perhaps also she weeps because the direct
physical apprehension of this "atom of balancing life" is
painful, as though Lawrence were saying here that to know
the world in the way of naked contact is painful at first for
those who have been "ravished by dead words become
obscene, and dead ideas become obsessions."

In the climax of this scene there is a reversal. Now it is
the gamekeeper who is "touched," who experiences a moment of overwhelming realization which leads him, despite
misgivings, to begin life anew, to become once again tender
and vulnerable and open in a world full of the sharp edges
and points of anti-vital abstractions and grim, uncontroll-
able machines.

In the hut to which the couple retire the woman asks
herself over and over again, "Was it real?" and, "Why
was this necessary?" but then deciding to lay down the burden of herself, she reflects that she is "to be had for the
taking." This phrase, so often employed cynically, expresses
here a change which is in the final analysis deeply spiritual
in implication. A lady yields her favors to a surly gamekeeper: a woman yields up herself to life and is saved. This
is an equation the novel as a whole insists upon and which
Lawrence's art attempts to sustain. The common experience
becomes charged with the most extraordinary significance

and the highest value life holds. This balance is perilous. To hold experience in this radiant and ennobling perspective is not an easy thing to do. Here, I think, the balance is maintained, and the reader can believe in what he sees.

Lawrence's last novel bears detailed and striking resemblances to his first, *The White Peacock*. Each has a gamekeeper, a wood, a lady who must choose between an industrial magnate and a "natural" man. But the two books contrast sharply in the way they turn out. In the earlier novel the lady chooses the magnate while the vital man sickens and dies. As a matter of fact, this pessimistic conclusion is doubled since no less than two men identified with the woods and fields, the farmer George Saxton and the gamekeeper Frank Annable, come to unhappy ends. But Mellors at the end of *Lady Chatterley's Lover* is still on his feet and, although gloomy enough about the future, can find the energy to set about planning a new life for himself and his mistress. Even in the letter which closes Lawrence's last novel, Mellors, despite his predictions of doom for modern industrial man, greets Connie hopefully and sets out his absurd program of salvation for the masses with conviction, if not with any idea that people are going to do what he suggests:

> If only they were educated to *live* instead of earn and spend, they could manage very happily on twenty-five shillings. If the men wore scarlet trousers as I said, they wouldn't think so much of money; if they could dance and hop and skip, and sing and swagger and be handsome, they could do with very little cash. And amuse the women themselves, and be amused by the women. They ought to learn to be naked and handsome, and to sing in a mass and dance the old group dances, and carve the stools they sit on, and embroider their own emblems. Then they wouldn't need money.　(p. 362)

This boyish and anarchic dream of peace on an earth magically transformed from the cold, crowded, and raw place that it by and large is—and was when people still danced group dances and hopped and skipped—into an innocent and sensual Garden rejects tragic knowledge of man's difficult position in the world. It flies in the face of facts. It is immature. Nevertheless, Lawrence was well aware that no one but a Laurentian gamekeeper could believe in such a program. He did not want men of the twentieth century to don white jackets and scarlet trousers pulled tight across the buttocks. But he did want men and women of the "tragic" age to look at themselves and to raise the question of whether the tragic view of man's plight took full account of creative human possibilities. He wanted us to look at our maturity and to consider whether it did not become for some people a mask concealing deadness.

The genuine yet carefully restrained optimism of *Lady Chatterley's Lover* is founded on a belief that the world is alive and that aliveness is the only thing worth cherishing. Men and societies denying this fundamental fact will sicken and die. In *The White Peacock* the gamekeeper had remarked, "Tell a woman not to come in a wood till she can look at natural things—she might see something." Connie Chatterley, unlike the heroine of *The White Peacock*, does come into the woods and lingers there until she sees something. More clearly and more persuasively than in any previous novel, Lawrence brings the reader into touch with that vision, the mystery which, as one suspected from the beginning, was only of life itself.

PART V

THE TALES

1

THE COMMON JUDGMENT that Lawrence's short stories and novellas contain a higher proportion of assured artistic successes than do his novels is substantially correct. One knows how to restore the faith of a reader who has bogged down halfway through *The Plumed Serpent* or fainted amid the profuse incremental repetitions of *The Rainbow*. Send him to "The Fox" or "Daughters of the Vicar" or "The Prussian Officer" or even "The Captain's Doll," and watch the brightness flow back into his eyes. Certainly, Lawrence is a great writer of the shorter tale, and if he is less than Chekhov he still has no equal among English writers, who have failed, by and large, to make their mark in this form. When we think of the modern short story in English we remember Hemingway and Joyce, perhaps Faulkner, Fitzgerald, Katharine Anne Porter, and Sean O'Faolain. But the scope, originality, and poise of Lawrence's stories establish him as a more considerable figure than any of these non-English writers, and this is worth emphasizing, since, in a purely insular context, Lawrence's title to pre-eminence is apt to be conferred by an embarrassing default.

And yet, this is not to suggest that Lawrence's shorter fiction taken as a whole is more valuable than his work in the novel. Literary value is determined not only by the achievements of formal discipline but also by the scale and size of what is attempted and done. Lawrence's ten novels are in the nature of a continuous speculation or experiment. He is constantly pushing beyond old limits, with respect to both feeling and form. As he alternately gropes and races toward radically new conclusions he is like an explorer who must move tirelessly across his newly discovered territory in order to establish its extent and claim it for his own. Once crossed and claimed the land becomes amenable to settlement, domestication, and finely scaled map-making. If the novels are Lawrence's major exploration of human reality, his lonely and at times heroic (and at times murky) vision of a land unknown, the tales represent just such settlement and domestication. They fill in behind the advancing frontier and turn virgin land into neighborhoods.

There is no doubt that the shorter fiction contains less strained argument and fewer lapses into uncertainty or confusion; that Lawrence was frequently able to effect a more direct release of his peculiarly rich sense of life within "disciplined limits"; that he moved easily within those limits whether he had in hand a mere sketch of half a dozen pages or a near-novel like "St. Mawr." Nevertheless, we need to make certain discriminations: to set aside the work that is merely good, or primarily interesting in its relation to Lawrence's autobiography or to his doctrines, in order to appreciate how much remains that is great and unique.

As one reads through the three volumes of short stories and the two volumes of short novels in the Phoenix Edition it is rather easy to group many of the tales according to reasonably distinct categories; yet, as might be expected, it is the best work that finally eludes the simple category. One group can be put together from the several stories which read as suggestive footnotes to certain of the novels. The most weirdly interesting of these is the early "The Shades of Spring," describing the return to his home valley of one John Syson, a young man who, like Paul Morel, had courted and then left a girl living on a farm. But this Miriam—her name is Hilda—has solaced herself in the arms of a local gamekeeper with whom she makes passionate love in a forest hut draped with the skins of wild animals.

There are enough references to the past to show that Syson's former relation to this girl was cast in the same mold as the unhappy, inhibited affair of Paul and Miriam. Yet where Miriam remained passive and spiritual Hilda has become bold and sensual, with no interest in returning to Syson. He had considered her "all spirit," but she now considers herself "like a plant. I can only grow in my own soil." "Shades of Spring" is a kind of arch which ties together the erotic dilemma of *Sons and Lovers* and the final solution of the dilemma in *Lady Chatterley*. We may want to conclude that Lawrence, after all, had only one story to tell, which he went on reworking until the ending came right, but a more reasonable inference is that the Miriam figure was from the beginning much more a plastic imaginative construct than a mere travesty of Lawrence's childhood sweetheart Jessie Chambers.

A second category, consisting of a half dozen or so stories that make fun of or otherwise discomfit certain people in the Lawrence circle, may be passed by quickly. "None of That" travesties Mabel Dodge's lust for willed experience and imagines a more sordid outcome to her career than the actual tough-minded woman would ever have tolerated. No less than four stories—"Smile," "The Border Line," "Jimmy and the Desperate Woman," and "The Last Laugh"—are aimed with some malice at J. Middleton Murry, the man to whom Lawrence most frequently assigned the role of Judas in the tragi-comedy of his relations with friends. "Things" distressed the American expatriate couple Earl and Achsah Brewster by exposing the materialism implicit in American upper-bohemian veneration of European antiquity, but these kind people still managed to remain on good terms with Lawrence to the very end of his life.

A third category consists of a few works of substantial

length which remain ambitious failures, owing either to excessive schematism in the ideas underlying the story, or indifferent success in the attempt to represent fictionally states of being about which Lawrence was confused or perverse. "The Ladybird" (*pace* Dr. Leavis) is, stylistically, Lawrence's ugliest story; its concern with "mastery" suggests that it issued from the same unwholesome region of Lawrence's imagination in which the leadership novels had developed. The hero, Count Dionys Psanek, is a lineal descendant of Dracula, except that, like Mr. Bela Lugosi, he stultifies where he intends to thrill.

"The Woman Who Rode Away," although it contains some of Lawrence's most brilliant renderings of landscape, is, like *The Plumed Serpent*, a heartless tale *au fond*. Both the Woman and Constance Chatterley "throw themselves away," the latter in the direction of renewed life, the former merely into an abyss of senseless blood sacrifice. The Woman's ritual disembowelment by Mexican Indians seeking to recover the power of command they have lost to gringos is neither excusable nor interesting; and the story contains one of the most depressing images in all Lawrence: a blonde woman crawling on hands and knees along a narrow mountain ledge, while her two Indian captors walk easily erect, one before, one behind, both indifferent to her discomfort and danger.

"The Man Who Died" is a near-success until the baroque conceit of "I am risen!" destroys the suspension of disbelief required for Lawrence's bold attempt to merge his own and the Christian myth of bodily resurrection. Analogous difficulties crop up in a spirit story like "Glad Ghosts." The lady ghost here remains too involved in problems of the life of the senses to persuade us that she is as other-worldly as the convention demands. She is apt to remind the reader of the last, unfinished canto of Byron's *Don Juan*, where

Juan mistakes for a phantom a warm, nubile lady wearing a sheet.

One of the most clear-cut groups among Lawrence's short stories consists of "Two Blue Birds," "The Lovely Lady," "Mother and Daughter," "Rawdon's Roof," and "The Blue Moccasins." These are united by their rather bitchy, facetious tone. The characters are middle- and upper-middle-class English people, and a recurring figure in several of these stories is the strong-minded, aging woman who has fastened herself parasitically onto someone younger and less clever than herself. Without abandoning his characteristic concern for vitality Lawrence successfully exploits here a talent for comedy of manners which he rarely employs in his novels. There is nothing to urge against these stories except that they are a bit too brittle and slight compared to his best work.

I could continue this categorizing—for example, the early stories of working-class life, the three thoroughly unsuccessful stories about sexual conflict set in or near London and obviously written during Lawrence's first years in London ("The Old Adam," "The Witch A La Mode," "New Eve and Old Adam")—except that I am much less interested in my schemes as such than to suggest what a large body of first-rate work remains after the ground has been cleared of work that is merely interesting, flawed, or only good enough to have made the international reputation of a lesser writer. It would take a separate book to discuss adequately the full range of Lawrence's short fiction. But I do have space to give, quite arbitrarily, what I take to be the canon of Lawrence's very best tales; and to select from the list two short stories and two short novels for some detailed commentary.

In the short story Lawrence's finest achievements are: "Odour of Chrysanthemums," "The Prussian Officer,"

"The Thorn in the Flesh," "Daughters of the Vicar," "The Shadow in the Rose Garden," "The Blind Man," "The Horse-Dealer's Daughter," "The Princess" (a marginal case), "The Man Who Loved Islands," "The Rocking Horse Winner." And among the short novels the best are: "Love Among the Haystacks," "The Fox," "The Captain's Doll," "St. Mawr" (another marginal case), "The Virgin and the Gypsy." By calling these Lawrence's best tales I mean to place them on a par with, say, "Byezhin Meadow," "In the Ravine," "The Death of Ivan Ilych," "A Simple Heart," "The Dead," "Bartleby the Scrivener," "Young Goodman Brown," and "The Light of the World."

2

I have chosen "Odour of Chrysanthemums," "The Man Who Loved Islands," "The Fox," and "The Virgin and the Gypsy" because they are personal favorites; because they are fairly well distributed over the range of Lawrence's nineteen-year publishing career; and because they make a wide spectrum of story types within the loose, well-nigh indefinable category of the "tale." All fit Pound's famous dictum for significant modern art. They "make it new," thereby reanimating and enlarging the imaginative scope of the story form. Also, each expresses a fundamental trend or theme in Lawrence's fiction as a whole. The first tale locates in the lives of working people trapped within the industrial system those irreducible human elements which define the characters' worth and dignity beyond the contingencies of class or system. The second treats "essentially" and intensively that drama of self-disintegration which, in the world of Lawrence's fiction, corresponds to the action of tragic or evil fate. The third is a mythical work of art enacting the "vast, unexplored morality of life itself" with enormous power and suggestiveness. The fourth uses a story archetype common to several of Lawrence's narratives to celebrate a triumph of wholesome impulse over diseased ways of living and for once this triumph does not lead toward alienation and isolation from the surrounding society.

The opening paragraph of "Odour of Chrysanthemums," first published in 1911, establishes a tension which is expressed everywhere in Lawrence's work but always most movingly in the setting of his own native Midlands:

The small locomotive engine, Number 4, came clanking, stumbling down from Selston with seven full wagons. It appeared round the corner with loud threats of speed, but the colt that it startled from among the gorse, which still flickered indistinctly in the raw afternoon, out-distanced it at a canter. A woman, walking up the railway line to Underwood, drew back into the hedge, held her basket aside, and watched the footplate of the engine advancing. The trucks thumped heavily past, one by one, with slow inevitable movement, as she stood insignificantly trapped between the jolting black wagons and the hedge; then they curved away towards the coppice where the withered oak leaves dropped noiselessly, while the birds, pulling at the scarlet hips beside the track, made off into the dusk that had already crept into the spinney. In the open, the smoke from the engine sank and cleaved to the rough grass. The fields were dreary and forsaken, and in the marshy strip that led to the whimsey, a reedy pit-pond, the fowls had already abandoned their run among the alders to roost in the tarred fowl-house. The pit-bank loomed up beyond the pond, flames like red sores licking its ashy sides, in the afternoon's stagnant light. Just beyond rose the tapering chimneys and the clumsy black headstocks of Brinsley Colliery. The two wheels were spinning fast up against the sky, and the winding engine rapped out its little spasms. The miners were being turned up. (*The Complete Short Stories*, II, 283)

The principle of composition here is simple contrast, the whole suffused, like the last stanza of Keats's ode "To Autumn," in an atmosphere of diminishment and decline. We see colt against locomotive engine, jolting wagons against flying birds, pit bank against pond, black headstocks against the dying light of an autumnal afternoon sky; we hear the clanking, jolting, spasmodic sounds of machinery against evening quiet; we sense the contrast between the bound, repetitive movements of locomotive wheels or lift machinery and the free movement in flight of animals and birds. These arrayed contrasts between machinery and a natural setting, embodying a tension between the necessity of human survival which called the industrial system into existence and the instinct of all living things to maintain themselves freely in being, are disturbed by one anomalous feature. A woman stands motionless, trapped between track and hedge, neither free to take flight like the animals, nor bound into a steely pattern of mechanical movement like the locomotive. She disappears immediately from the story but the anomaly of this human entrapment remains and becomes the central, moving motive of the story.

The drab cottage of Elizabeth Bates, clutched by its bony vine and with its long garden containing a few apple trees and some failing chrysanthemums, presses up against the cinder roadbed of the line. The mother is tall, straight, handsome, and fruitful, and she is also tense, unhappy, and exhausted because of her collier husband's evening visits to the pub, with their inevitable consequence, a further reduction of the scanty housekeeping allowance. The family atmosphere, established by the scene of the supper and the talk between brother, sister, and mother, is warm and close, and includes the father, whose inexplicably prolonged absence on this particular evening is concretely felt by all three.

Yet this atmosphere is also suffused with a permanent tension. The mother's inevitable anger at her husband's fecklessness, like the miner's drinking bouts, continues from day to day, and the children react anxiously to both these disturbing features of the shared life of the family. Finally, the husband, although we never see him alive, is a figure of anomaly. On the one hand his life is bound in with the rhythms of the machine; for he descends into the mine and returns to the surface according to the rigid patterns of a work schedule; and perhaps the machine principle has even invaded his "free" time, since the drinking habits of workmen are at least partially determined by the overfatigue and boredom consequent on heavy industrial labor. On the other hand, his mother remembers the warm laugh, perfect health, and high animal spirits he had had as a boy. His wife has laid her "living flesh" against his and out of these conjunctions have come children and a child as yet unborn—new life that is unbound, unpredictable, alive with possibility.

In the central scene of the story—the account of the laying out and washing of the miner's dead body by Elizabeth and her mother-in-law—we seem to pass beyond these contradictions:

"You must help me now," she whispered to the old woman. Together they stripped the man.

When they arose, saw him lying in the naive dignity of death, the women stood arrested in fear and respect. For a few moments they remained still, looking down, the old mother whimpering. Elizabeth felt countermanded. She saw him, how utterly inviolable he lay in himself. She had nothing to do with him. She could not accept it. Stooping,

she laid her hand on him, in claim. He was still warm, for
the mine was hot where he had died. His mother had his
face between her hands, and was murmuring incoherently.
The old tears fell in succession as drops from wet leaves; the
mother was not weeping, merely her tears flowed. Elizabeth
embraced the body of her husband, with cheek and lips.
She seemed to be listening, inquiring, trying to get some
connection. But she could not. She was driven away. He
was impregnable.   (II, 299)

In this most moving of all the scenes in Lawrence's fiction Elizabeth, and the reader, seem to recover a Blakeian
true vision of the fundamental, living reality of a man.
But it is illusory. He *has* been violated. His warmth is from
the mine. He is dead. Yet the image of this inviolable reality lingers, and tortures Elizabeth in her grief as she reflects that she had never known him, or he known her.
They had denied each other fundamentally. "And this had
been her life and his life. She was grateful to death, which
restored the truth."

The story's image of life in the industrial age is that of
a sickly, autumnal flower growing beside a cinder track
and appearing first in association with pregnancy—Elizabeth puts chrysanthemums in the band of her apron—finally
in association with death. But we must be careful about this
change. The flower is sickly, yet it has grown by itself until
picked and will grow again. Bates's death restores the truth
which the anomalous and alienating features of the industrial
system have covered up. With perfect objectivity and compassion Lawrence describes a waste of life in order to affirm
life and discriminates the point from which civilization must
begin to reconstruct itself if we wish to recover a true,
unanomalous vision of ourselves, one another, and the
world. And this point is a recognition of the naive, inviolable, impregnable dignity of an ordinary workman laid out

on the floor of a miner's cottage, his life wasted, the lives of his family blighted, his cooling body prepared for burial.

"The Man Who Loved Islands," first published in 1928, is perhaps Lawrence's greatest story in what may be called the fable or parable form. In such narratives—"The Man Who Died" and "The Rocking Horse Winner" are other notable examples—Lawrence solved the problem of dealing effectively with special states of being and awareness by dispensing with much of the realistic machinery he customarily employed in his longer novels. The action of these stories is set at a carefully calculated distance from the world of contemporary civilization. Their characters are simplified figures who epitomize particular aspects of the human condition in relatively pure form. Their greatness lies in the fact that, while they embody familiar Laurentian assumptions usually represented as a mixture of realism and symbolism in most of the longer novels, these stories never emerge as flat allegories, and their characters manage to remain fully expressive and alive.

F. R. Leavis, in speaking of this kind of Lawrence narrative, uses the word "frame-effect" to designate what I have referred to as a fable or parable quality in the form. The frame-effect limits "the freedom of the reader's implicit reference from the world of the tale to the expectations and habits of ordinary everyday actuality."[1] This explanation is valuable because it does not assume there is no connection between the story and ordinary life; it assumes only that the reader must not expect ready and obvious connections. In "The Man Who Loved Islands" the reader's stock expectations are inhibited from the opening sentence onward. This sentence—"There was a man who loved islands"—by itself evokes the formalized world of the

[1] *D. H. Lawrence, Novelist* (New York: Knopf, 1956), p. 56.

fairy tale. A man with a peculiar passion is summoned into existence by an apparently naive narrator, and as the story unfolds, this passion is everything, and the only thing, the narrator tells us about. The passion is the story's premise, just as the continuously expanding lust of the fisherman's wife for power and riches is the premise of the well-known folk tale. Both stories concern themselves with effects; there is little direct inquiry into the causes of these consuming passions, although by the time one has finished "The Man Who Loved Islands" he is in a position to construct for himself the kind of previous experience which brought the hero to the point of indulging in his fatal ambition to possess fully an island.

Before proceeding to a closer inspection of Lawrence's story, we need to say something more about the position of the narrator. He keeps the story in his own hands, rejecting the temptation to render the action as a series of extended scenes, and he never moves away from his hero to take up a position close to some other character for any significant period of time. His attitude toward the hero is occasionally tinged with irony, but the ironic tone tends to drop away as the islander moves deeper and deeper into his quixotic condition. The narrator's main effort is directed at making the reader see the world through the eyes of his perverse hero. This means that other people in the story remain shadowy figures—because the hero sees them as shadows—and that the real drama takes place within an increasingly morbid consciousness. In every possible way then, the story withdraws the reader from the world "as it is." But as long as morbid consciousnesses remain a part of what men encounter in their dealings with the world, this story will continue to illuminate reality.

The action of "The Man Who Loved Islands" represents the disintegration of a self. This fate is brought on by the

hero's steadily accelerating withdrawal from those relationships with the surrounding world which, on Lawrence's
view, determine the health and integrity of any human
being. The story's development may be described as the
continual shrinking of a circle around another circle, until
the inner circle of the self and the outer circle of the non-
self nearly coincide at that moment just before death with
which the story concludes. Alternatively, it may be described as the systematic, willed reduction of the varied colors of experience to the flat whiteness of death-in-life, that
peculiar Laurentian simulacrum of being in which the isolated ego dissolves into pure abstractedness. In the final
third of the story the hero becomes Faust in reverse, a rapt
soul who attempts to diminish the universe to a dimension-
less point, who tries to conquer otherness by thinking its
modes of space and time out of existence. In his final cold
agonies there is something magnificent about Cathcart. The
grandeur of his presumption against life compels awe from
the reader even as he recognizes the justness of his failure.

There can be no doubt that Cathcart does fail, even on
his own terms. He has tried to replace the phenomenal
world by an idea, which in the beginning is no more than
the idea of himself, and in the end is only the idea of a
cold blankness. But before he can annihilate the "elements,"
these elements rush in to annihilate him. Before he can dis-
pose of the living universe, he is pushed out of life by the
monstrous snows his vision has evoked. This insular egoist
will die digging his way to the lifeboat not because he desires to live but because "if he was to be shut in, it must
be by his own choice, not by the mechanical power of the
elements." The snows have interrupted his experiment in
reduction, his search for an apotheosis of nonbeing. The
world forces on him human definition and a human fate

just as he seems on the point of escaping from the human condition:

> He looked stupidly over the whiteness of his foreign island, over the waste of the lifeless sea. He pretended to imagine he saw the wink of a sail. Because he knew too well there would never again be a sail on that stark sea.
> As he looked, the sky mysteriously darkened and chilled. From far off came the mutter of the unsatisfied thunder, and he knew it was the signal of the snow rolling over the sea. He turned, and felt its breath on him.
> (*The Complete Short Stories*, III, 746)

These are the story's final lines. The implication is clear that Cathcart cannot survive a third encounter with the snow. However, it is imaginable that he is already dead. He is in a cold hell of his own making, caught forever in the moment of terrible awareness when he recognizes how his will to eliminate life from his reckoning has been thwarted. This is his frozen apotheosis, his eternal fate, to look forever across a lifeless sea and to grasp—this man who has striven after utter unrelatedness with the world— the fatal connection between himself and the smothering element of snow.

Cathcart and his fate are Lawrence's most concentrated image of the disease of human idealism. There is a generic resemblance between the islander and certain characters in the novels who exhibit the disruption of the organic bond and the tendency to attempt the subjugation of the phenomenal world to the abstracted will and intellect. For Lawrence, thought itself seems at times to become identical with egoism. The man with ideas always imposes abstractions on the concrete, the absolute on the contingent, the word on life. In the end, processes of abstraction are viewed as monstrous processes of self-assertion. Thus, in *The First*

Lady Chatterley the platonizing Sir Clifford digests his wife into pure idea.

> For he himself was absolute in all his universe, and she was a thing to be made use of. His immortality, his heaven of pure truth, the pure ideal, the pure light, it was only himself in his oneness exalted to an absolute and everything but himself fused away. No room for her, no room for anything. If she were there in the final white glare of his heaven, she would be so fused down that she was gone, gone entirely, become a pure part of him in his final transfiguration. (p. 75)

Thought, this seems to be saying, is egoism. Ideals, things of the spirit, are self-exaltation. The man of ideals is the supreme egotist in whose orbit real things become fused down into pure idea, an idea which in the end is no more than the thinker's idea of himself. Lawrence in the same book calls this process a "white abomination of tyranny." White is symbolically the color of the disembodied will, intellect, the ideal. It is associated with purity and lifelessness. In the story under consideration white is a pervasive symbolic color (or absence of color), as from one point of view "The Man Who Loved Islands" is a symbolic enactment of the Laurentian critique of idealism. The story detaches the idealist from an elaborate social context and permits him to carry his abstracting tendency to a fantastic climax. Cathcart belongs not only with Chatterley but also with Gerald Crich. The dramatization of Gerald's death in the alpine snows at the end of *Women in Love* is a symbolic action which foreshadows—foreblanches might be an appropriate coinage here—Cathcart's white immolation on his third island.

But there is an important difference between Cathcart and the other two figures. Crich and Chatterley are industrialists. Their idealism involves an imposition of abstracted, mechanized patterns of toil upon their flesh-and-blood workmen. Cathcart's self-imposition is at once less harmful to the mass of mankind and more destructive in its aspirations. He stands in the same relation to the industrialists as the pure to the applied scientist. Ultimately, he wants nothing less than to tyrannize over the universe, and after he has moved to the third island he asks no recognition from the world he is absorbed in fusing down into nothingness.

As we watch him come apart in the story's final pages, we are apt to forget the perverse splendor of his aspirations and to assume that he suffers with the disintegration of his humanness. But no cry of despair ever issues from this great life-denier. He has become so accustomed to the "quaking and writhing of his body" that he hardly notices it, and his final utterance as he looks out at the snow hills on his island—"It is summer, and the time of leaves"—poetically expresses the essence of his mad vision, the genius of his negation. He is one figure in the Laurentian gallery who can hold his own in an age when devoted, brilliant men expend their intellectual powers in the effort to translate abstracted descriptions of the living universe given by the equations of contemporary physical theory into weapons capable of destroying all life on the earth's surface. Indeed, the only bar to Cathcart's final success would have been removed if he had possessed an arsenal of hydrogen bombs.

Cathcart himself is the principal symbol of "The Man Who Loved Islands," and the island settings are, on one level, images or mirror reflections of his thought. We apprehend his essence by studying descriptions of his surroundings. Conventional distinctions between inner and outer worlds dissolve as Cathcart purchases a series of miniature universes that he can "presume to fill . . . with [his] own personality." As this personality progressively deteriorates under its burden of disconnectedness, he moves deeper and deeper into abstraction. His ghastly metamorphoses of self are evidenced through differences in the appearance of successive islands. The first contains some miles of fertile, flowery, sea-encircled earth, the last some rods of bleak, snow-covered reef. A comparison of descriptions of landscape becomes a comparison of three conditions of a soul:

> Our islander loved his island very much. In early spring, the little ways and glades were a snow of blackthorn, a vivid white among the Celtic stillness of close green and grey rock, blackbirds calling out in the whiteness their first long, triumphant calls. After the blackthorn and the nestling primroses came the blue apparition of hyacinths, like elfin lakes and slipping sheets of blue, among the bushes and under the glade of trees. And many birds with nests you could peep into, on the island all your own. Wonderful what a great world it was!
>
> Followed summer, and the cowslips gone, the wild roses faintly fragrant through the haze. There was a field of hay, the foxgloves stood looking down. In a little cove, the sun was on the pale granite where you bathed, and the shadow was in the rocks. Before the mist came stealing, you went home through the ripening oats, the glare of the sea fading from the high air as the fog-horn started to moo on the other island. And then the sea-fog went, it was autumn, the oat-sheaves lying prone, the great moon, another island, rose golden out of the sea, and rising higher, the world of the sea was white.   (III, 723; Island I)

> On this island there were no human ghosts, no ghosts of any ancient race. The sea, and the spume and the weather, had washed them all out, washed them out so there was only the sound of the sea itself, its own ghost, myriad-voiced, communing and plotting and shouting all winter long. And only the smell of the sea, with a few bristly bushes of gorse and coarse tufts of heather, among the grey, pellucid rocks, in the grey, more-pellucid air. The coldness, the greyness,

even the soft, creeping fog of the sea, and the islet of rock
humped up in it all, like the last point in space.

(III, 734; Island II)

And now it continued, day after day, a dull, deathly cold.
Occasional crumblings of snow were in the air. The days
were greyly longer, but no change in the cold. Frozen grey
daylight. The birds passed away, flying away. Some he saw
lying frozen. It was as if all life were drawing away,
contracting away from the north, contracting south-
wards. . . .

He woke in the morning to a curious whiteness. His
window was muffled. It had snowed. He got up and opened
his door, and shuddered. Ugh! how cold! All white, with a
dark leaden sea, and black rocks curiously speckled with
white. The foam was no longer pure. It seemed dirty. And
the sea ate at the whiteness of the corpse-like land.

(III, 744; Island III)

A decline of color, of lively rhythms, of variety in the
objects represented is obvious as we move from the first
passage to the third. Really it is the movement from life
into death. It should be noted, however, that even the first
description, through its references to the white moon and
white sea, pale granite and stealing mist, suggests a pre-
dominating pallor which conveys the hero's first degree of
alienation from the phenomenal world.

My statement that the settings function as symbolic mir-
rors of Cathcart's inward condition fails to indicate an important contradiction. Cathcart makes his world conform
to his idealizing thought—to his image of himself—only
up to a point. Behind the islands of his fantasy lurk real
islands which cannot be transformed by any idea, and it is
the malevolence of the real that drives him deeper and
deeper into himself. Only the third island, by its very nature aspiring to a condition of blankness and pointlessness,

seems to present no challenge to the hero's inner world. This treeless and unpopulated wasteland, once he has stripped it of its sheep, contains nothing to interfere with his presumptuous dream of making some part of the external world "a world of his own," or his desire to fill an island with his personality—except that now he has no personality, and, as we have seen, the elements remain. Emptiness within is echoed by emptiness without until the snow drops a curtain on this morose comedy.

On the first island Cathcart does possess a personality. He is a man ridden by fantasies of perfection, a man incapable of establishing real connections with others, but he is not yet the wraithlike figure he later is to become. His failure here to establish his dream as fact stems from the absurdity of the dream itself. Practically, he is trying to run a farming enterprise which will pay for itself, thereby enabling him to ignore the rest of the world. But his workmen betray him, and the island itself betrays him because he is not in touch with things as they are. He envisions himself as the Master who strolls through an earthly paradise teeming with fertility and populated by faithful hinds. As he walks about in his "creamy-white serge" suits, his graceful hands making gestures of "white emphasis," he is dramatizing himself as the god of a self-contained world.

In actual fact, however, his employees are highly discontented, while out of the island's air comes a "stony, heavy malevolence," a malice expressing itself in the series of uncanny accidents which befall his workers, his crops, and his livestock. The island is removed spatially from the rest of the world, but the Master discovers to his horror that the island cannot be detached from "worlds of undying time," past worlds of savage human experience which are a part of the land's living heritage. The point behind all this is that you cannot impose mind on nature. The island possesses its own reality and its own spirit. To master an island one must begin with what is there, not with an egocentric dream of perfection.

On the second island Cathcart has lost much of his sentimentality. The place is to be a refuge rather than a world. In a very important metaphorical sense the second island represents a midpoint in the hero's career. Here he enters into a "strange stillness from all desire." His face assumes a "gossamy look"; he says to himself: "I am turned into a dream. I feel nothing." Island I represented an egoistic assertion. Island III represents a transcendent act of negation. Between these, Island II expresses neither a plus nor a minus. It is a zero point. Descriptively, it emerges as a prevailing greyness, misty, without ghosts, its damp air echoing with the myriad, indistinct voices of the sea. Cathcart's spirit is here described as a "dim-lit cave under water, where strange sea-foliage expands upon the watery atmosphere. . . . All still and soft and uncrying, yet alive as rooted seaweed is alive." He is driven from this still point of living nonattachment by the last challenge that ever reaches him from the human world. His affair with Flora presents the hero a final opportunity to link himself up among the living. It is the failure of this relationship— a willed failure on his part—which drives him to sever himself altogether from the world and its people.

On the third island, as I have already suggested, Cathcart's personality has dissolved. There is nothing in him but a fixed will to pass beyond the limits of the phenomenal world. He is consumed by a horror not only of living things but even of shapes, colors, and sounds. He watches the sea because it is shapeless, pale, and quiet. His mind turns "soft and hazy, like the hazy ocean." He hates his sheep, his cat, and the fishermen who visit to supply him with the necessities of life because his mind is attempting to empty itself of all traces of a living world:

> Only he still derived his single satisfaction from being alone, absolutely alone, with the space soaking into him. The grey sea alone, and the footing of his sea-washed island. No other contact. Nothing human to bring its horror into contact with him. Only space, damp, twilit, sea washed space! This was the bread of his soul.   (III, 742-743)

During his final days Cathcart eats dried milk and malt, a lifeless and blanched food, and comes even to despise that last refuge of the idealist, the printed word, because it reminds him of the "depravity of speech."

In the end Cathcart no doubt becomes a madman, but the story hardly permits the reader to dismiss the central figure as a harmless maniac. His disease is mind-derived, and he finishes by destroying only himself. Given other circumstances, the same ghastly habit of mind could ravage the entire civilized world. It was, of course, Lawrence's deep conviction that the ravages of the abstracted intelligence and will were evident throughout modern experience, corrupting the friendships, loves, and working associations of men and women everywhere. Cathcart is mad in that he does not take the world as it is into his reckoning. The mind, isolated from living truth, can create only deadness; and living truth for Lawrence involves the recognition that the only marvel is to be alive in the flesh, and to be linked up in a universe which is organically alive.

"The Man Who Loved Islands" dramatizes a modern habit of mind, the habitual assumption of the modern civilized man that the relations between the individual and his world are a matter of words and ideas, that organic ties do not exist. Lawrence is saying here, as he has said elsewhere, that man imposes his abstracted thought upon life at the cost of his own life, that we must live with rather than against the life teeming in and around us.

The art of "The Man Who Loved Islands" is well-nigh flawless. The fable of Cathcart and his islands sums up everything Lawrence has to say about the perniciousness of the abstract without rage, without faltering, without argument. The complete story is what Robert Frost calls a "constant symbol"[2] of its meaning. Its descriptions evoke the beauty of the phenomenal world and the horrific emptiness of a world subdued to the irreverent mind of a man who aspires to a godlike condition but who cannot feel love for or connection with any created thing. This story, unlike so many of Lawrence's narratives, leaves no questions suspended at its close. Perhaps this suggests that Lawrence's prophetic vision of doom for modern man was more powerful than his vision of hope. Really, it does not matter. As the artist who could create a tale like "The Man Who Loved Islands," he transcends the limitations of the prophet and works a permanent change in the thought and feeling of his reader.

"The Fox," published in 1921, presents an artistically subtle and emotionally powerful version of the Laurentian success story. A vital relation is achieved for one character and preserved for another when Henry Grenfel succeeds in breaking Jill Banford's hold over Nellie March, thereby separating the latter from an unnatural, unwholesome way of life. The principal situation recalls both *The Lost Girl* and *Lady Chatterley's Lover*. Henry, like Cicio and Mellors in the longer novels, intrudes upon a relationship which, in the eyes of the conventional world, is perfectly decent.

[2] See *The Poems of Robert Frost: With an Introductory Essay "The Constant Symbol" by the Author* (New York: Modern Library, 1946), pp. xv-xxiv.

He is a man without social status, uncouth and uneducated. The two women are hardly his social superiors, but they have made for themselves a living arrangement which reflects some pretensions to culture. March paints white swans on porcelain; they have a piano and an oriental rug. They plume themselves on the fact that they are something better than mere farmers. In the long evenings at the isolated house they try to forget the unmastered problems of the daily farm routine, the chickens which will not lay, the depredations of a demonic fox who supplies the story with its key symbol, their difficulties with a heifer who will not stay penned and with another heifer who is expecting her first calf.

Up to a point this situation is comic, the humor resting on a simple ironic incongruity or contradiction. These women do not possess the physical energy and skills which farming demands. Furthermore, as females they are incapable of making a total commitment of themselves to this traditionally masculine work. The farm desperately needs a man. March, despite her masculine garb and cabinet-making skill, cannot cure the sick chickens or protect them from the fox. The two women are performing a travesty of farming, just as in their personal lives they are performing a travesty of marriage.

With this description of the two women's personal relationship we pass beyond comedy and enter an area where a more disturbing contradiction is evident. The farming enterprise, while fantastically unsuccessful, is at least sanctioned by the shortage of male agricultural laborers in England during wartime. But the mock marriage these women enact violates the instinctive economy of life itself. The friendship is unfertile and unproductive, like the farm. It is a metaphor of the condition of death-in-life comparable to the relationship of Lady Chatterley and her crippled

husband or the drab connections which bind Alvina Houghton to her family, her town, and her sympathetic nerve-
worn friend, Miss Frost.

When Henry Grenfel challenges this sterile connection,
he carries matters swiftly to a climax of violence; but even
before he appears it is evident that March, like both Alvina
and Lady Chatterley and unlike her devitalized friend, is
not beyond rescue. As in the longer novels, these leading actors can be fitted into a kind of hierarchy. Henry is fully
and instinctively alive. Banford at the other extreme is
altogether dead, while March is altogether divided between
death and life. She is the prize over whom two utterly opposed individuals struggle, the Persephone figure who may
be raped either into death or life. Henry and Banford represent two different forms of will. Backing one is the force
of instinct, backing the other the force of convention and
conformity. Of course the conclusion is foregone, just as the
final unresolved question of how Henry Grenfel and his
captive bride will manage to settle themselves in life seems
inevitable.

"The Fox" is admirable because it compels the reader's
belief in the conflict both as narrative fact and as symbol,
compels through its swiftness and economy, its violence, its
uncanniness, its integration. There is nothing in Lawrence's
novels to compare with "The Fox's" denouement, and nothing, really, to compare with the subtle interweaving of the
fox symbol through a series of plausibly realistic episodes.
When Henry murders Banford the reader is made aware
that this story risks more, and in surviving that risk, achieves
more than many of Lawrence's fictions. A loutish returned
soldier kills a poor, defenseless woman cunningly, so that
he cannot be brought to trial for a capital crime. Then he
runs off with her friend, another defenseless woman so

shattered by the experience of witnessing the bloody death that she cannot further resist his crude solicitations.

In this summary "The Fox" sounds like a sordid episode taking place in society's lower depths, part of that dreary modern folklore which treats of the agonies precipitated when the warrior retraces his steps from the trenches of World War I to the peaceful but hardly innocent land he has defended, bringing his habit of violence to bear upon the civilian scene. This, of course, is not what the story is about. Its image of life's essentials agrees at no point with this summary. Henry's act is not a murder. It is an inspired and creative deed. To be able to say this one must recognize that the story, through the way that it is told, is unusually successful in bringing the reader's responses into line with Lawrence's own visionary perspective.

"The Fox" in some sense begins, continues, and ends as a realistic drama with believable characters who interact in a pattern of plausible, logically concatenated events. Yet somehow it modulates into a symbolic drama or fable where the ultimate issues of life and death confront each other until an inevitable resolution is reached. When Henry Grenfel drops a dead tree on Jill Banford, the reader reflects that the boy has merely employed one dead thing to sweep another dead thing out of life's way.

It is an indication of Lawrence's firm artistic control that the reader can accept without reservation this nominally horrifying incident as an image of the triumph of life over death; for it means that a vision of reality has conquered the banality of the nominally and conventionally real. Places in Lawrence's fiction where he tests the underlying motives of human interaction adequately on the plane of realistic action are rare. We find murder more often in the metaphor than in the dramatic situation. Here the eruption of violence in the quiet English countryside seems salutary. It validates that inner drama of souls which sometimes in Lawrence's fiction bears only an attenuated connection with what his characters manage to do.

It is always harder to explain the achievement of a superior work of art than to point out the inadequacies of an artistic failure. Nevertheless, some elucidation is always possible. Here I should like to discuss how the story's setting, its modes of characterization, and its central, expanding symbol help to maintain that constant visionary focus on events which gives "The Fox" full power to win assent from its reader.

The most important thing about the story's setting is its very real isolation from the larger world of contemporary Britain. This lonely Berkshire farm, located at the edge of a wood and some miles from the nearest village, stands, as it were, at the margins of civilization, at a point where it is fully exposed to the uncanny powers which for Lawrence are assumed to lurk in wild nature. The wood, as in Lawrence's first and last novels, is a symbol of a nature uncorrupted by man's civilizing tendencies. It stands also for the life of the instincts, a mode of being shared by human and nonhuman creatures alike. Out of the wood comes the fox to steal chickens, but also to cast his spell over Nellie March. Henry Grenfel assumes the fox's qualities as the story moves along, but even without the symbolic connection he is identified with the woodland. Like Annable and Mellors he is a hunter, a man with a gun rather than a man with a hoe.

Given this suggestive location, the disparity between the life led indoors and the teeming of wild things in the nearby wood becomes crucial. In the face of nature the quasi-Lesbian *modus vivendi* of March and Banford cannot be rationalized. In Lawrence generally the vital imperative, an instinctive demand life makes upon men and women to link themselves up with the living whole, reaches his fictional characters in the dual form of threat and promise. If the character is too far gone in death, the threat fulfills itself; but if the character can be saved, then, after some preliminary agonies and *rites du passage*, the promise will be fulfilled. Here, with an uncharacteristic economy of means, a single pastoral figure, Henry Grenfel—"a piece of the out-of-doors come in-doors"—penetrates the stuffy little world the women have made for themselves and hunts down one for life, the other for death.

The dramatic conflict is sustained and made significant through its location at a midpoint between civilization and the wilderness. This location is the appropriate, almost necessary, ground for Lawrence to stage his attack on modern culture and his defense of natural mysteries. For a novel like *The Lost Girl* suggests that one cannot carry the out-of-doors into the heart of the industrial wasteland any more than one can carry water through a desert in a sieve. Foxes can harry outlying farms, but in the city they must skulk like any cur.

Characterization of the principal actors in "The Fox" skillfully combines two distinguishable modes into a unified presentation. First of all, the three characters possess personal and social traits reflecting conventional differences in background, in psychology, in experience of the world. Henry, Banford, and March talk like real people and respond to ordinary occurrences as anyone might in similar circumstances. It is plausible that two young women should try to run a farm for themselves after having had some experience as landgirls. It is plausible also that a young soldier who comes to the farm in search of his grandfather should linger out the time of his furlough in an attempt to make love to one of these apparently unattached women. The mimetic artistry of much of the dialogue is striking.

March's letter to Henry, expressing the rather witless charm of this sensitive yet dull-minded girl, is an especially fine piece of work, comparable as dramatic impersonation to Mrs. Bolton's remarkable gossiping monologue in Chapter IX of *Lady Chatterley's Lover*.

As an example of something more complex but still within the range of a realistic presentation, there is Banford's fit of hysterics over Henry's insistence that March walk outside with him the evening before he returns to camp. These social and psychological dimensions of character are developed largely through dialogue and dramatic scenes. In this way an objective character is established for each person. On the whole, this conventional sort of character definition is adequate but not very elaborate. Lawrence is not interested in presenting complexities of personal motivation or a really complicated interaction of character on the social plane of action.

Concurrent with this realism another mode of characterization is worked into the story which establishes a dimension of significance in the experiences of the individuals having little to do with social or psychological problems in the conflict situation. For two of the actors—Henry and March—it establishes a connection with the anti-social world of nature itself and through that connection a relation with each other which is fated, inevitable, and largely uncontrolled by the conscious predispositions each exhibits. Banford alone remains almost entirely uncharacterized through this second mode, and this is significant. Her social and psychological character are her essence. But this is not true of the lovers. When Henry appears in the story, he is already "linked up" in the organic sense as a vital human being; and March, within the first four pages, has succumbed to the possessive magic of the fox: "He had become a settled effect in her spirit, a state permanently established, not continuous, but always recurring." For these two an instinctive being exists, a being which underlies consciousness and what we conventionally call character.

Lawrence cannot establish this special quality of being as an operative factor in the story through dialogue and dramatic scenes. As we have seen earlier, the Laurentian essence does not lend itself to conventional representation. But it can be, and in this story is, created as a suggestion through imagery, metaphor, and symbol, and through highly metaphorical descriptions of unnamable feelings which surge through the living man and woman. Sometimes it is brought into the story through an intense and rich description of the character at some isolated moment when an unanalyzable realization enters consciousness. Often it is defined through an elaboration of surface details of descriptive imagery which, in their regular recurrence from one end of the story to another, come to function as signs of some inner meaning at best only partially analyzable.

It should be stressed that these descriptions never actually determine what is taking place in the inner consciousness of the character. Instead they continuously point at the existence of mysterious dynamisms without pretending to encompass what is in motion beneath the surface. Furthermore, the characters are quite incapable of communicating their deep awareness to one another in words. The love dialogue of March and Henry is a tissue of clichés. But in their looks, gestures, and in the images supplied by the narrator's descriptions the important communication is made.

After March has once seen the fox, she goes restlessly looking for him through the woods, gun in hand:

> For he had lifted his eyes upon her, and his knowing look seemed to have entered her brain. She did not so much think of him: she was possessed by him. She saw his dark,

shrewd, unabashed eye looking into her, knowing her. She felt him invisibly master her spirit. She knew the way he lowered his chin as he looked up, she knew his muzzle, the golden brown, and the greyish white. And again she saw him glance over his shoulder at her, half inviting, half contemptuous and cunning. So she went, with her great startled eyes glowing, her gun under her arm, along the wood edge. Meanwhile the night fell, and a great moon rose above the pine trees. And again Banford was calling.

(The Short Novels, I)

This is eerie enough, and we must recognize that the ways in which March knows the fox and the fox knows March are hardly amenable to analysis. But as the story moves on and passages with this quality of uncanniness turn up again and again, the reader's hold on the real is undermined. His limited expectations of what people may do and be are transformed. Surrendering himself to the power of imagery and metaphor he soon comes to view the action on its own terms. At the end he cannot find his way back to firm ground to express a condemnation of what in a less skillfully managed progression might have appeared to be an unsavory climax.

To say that a reader comes to understand the story on its own terms means not only that "The Fox" establishes its own radical pattern of morality, but also that there are to be found among the images, metaphors, and symbols patterns which express the underlying visionary theme. The fox symbol is of course the central example here, but it is not an isolated one. For instance, the narrator gives an extraordinarily large number of descriptions of the eyes of the three characters. At the beginning the fox establishes its power over March through a look which it gives her, and at the end of the story the same girl capitulates to Henry's will after Banford's death when she gazes up at him

with "a senseless look of helplessness and submission." Between these two references are a great many descriptions of
differences in the characteristic appearance of the eyes of
each character. These differences persist through all developments of the action. They convey in imagistic terms
an important underlying meaning.

March's eyes are invariably described as wide, dilated,
open. Frequently a contrast is drawn between the expression of her eyes and mouth. Her mouth is pursed, shrewish,
tight, compressed. This contrast of course reflects the conflict in her deepest nature between receptivity and negation.
She wants to remain loyal to her woman friend, but from
the beginning her eyes betray her. When Henry proposes
marriage to March, her words rebuff him rudely, but the
girl is usually under his spell as long as she can look directly
at him. She tries to break with him by letter after he has
passed out of sight, but when he reappears she is helpless.

Henry's eyes are described again and again as abnormally
bright, sharp, keen, penetrating, and searching. These ad-
jectives define his role in the story. He is the man who cuts
his way into the world of two women, who searches the
relationship with foxlike curiosity and cunning and sees
that it is doomed. His abnormally acute eyesight discovers
the fox slipping through the darkness, and it is at least as
much a tribute to his visual powers as to his skill with an
axe that he can drop the tree so unerringly on his female
rival. Banford, significantly enough, is near-sighted, wears
glasses, and cannot read books without her eyes rapidly becoming tired. She has "queer, round-pupilled, weak eyes
staring behind her spectacles." Unlike March's, her eyes
never glow, darken, or dilate. They are commonly described
as vague, hidden behind the spectacles, neither seeing nor
seen.

I dwell on this descriptive detail not because nothing like

it had ever been done in literature before but because such recurrences are an extremely important part of Lawrence's imaginative method. According to an old idea the eyes are a window to the soul. The little drama of looks enacted in "The Fox" is a clue to a drama of "souls" which goes on during the long evenings in the farm living room when the principal characters do little but stare at one another.

The fox, as a ubiquitous presence and unifying symbol, is one of Lawrence's most satisfying fictional devices. Perhaps better than any other writer of his time he knew how to describe animals and to suggest their characteristic traits without sentimentality. The power of the fox as symbol depends upon the vividness of the fox's presentation as animal. Its first appearance under March's startled eyes and its last, when it is hung up by the heels in the shed, provide an opportunity for exact, sensitive description of the animal in all its glory of full growth and in all the ineluctable mystery of its wildness. Like nature as a whole, the fox is beautiful yet terrifying, familiar yet unknowable.

Through most of the story the fox is not presented as a mysterious symbolic presence by the narrator himself. March's first encounter with it is described in terms appropriate to an hallucinatory experience, and it is March alone who transfers the qualities of the animal to the young man. Banford sees nothing of this, and the narrator does not labor the relation of the human intruder to the animal marauder in discursive terms. To March Henry has the smell of the fox, but to Banford Henry merely has an unpleasant odor. March's first dream, with its beautiful detail of the fox's singing and its fiery and terrifying climax, comes true for her, but the reader is left free to note a difference between a kiss on the lips and the scorching brush of a fox tail across a dreaming mouth. With the occurrence of the second dream, however, we pass beyond the readily explicable. March dreams that her beloved Banford is dead, "and the coffin was the rough woodbox in which the bits of chopped wood were kept in the kitchen, by the fire." When Banford is slain, it is by a dead tree chopped down for the kitchen fire. The dream in some sense predicts Banford's fate while simultaneously it follows the now classic pattern of the Freudian wish-fulfillment.

Once this question of the supernatural has been raised, the reader's firm assurance that the link between fox and man is not objectively "real" dissolves. But Lawrence does not press the point. Instead this fleeting glimpse of mystery simply influences the reader to explore the connections between animal and man in terms not narrowly circumscribed by the conventions of ordinary realism. A similar point can be made about Banford's connection with the woodbox. The second dream prepares us to see her demise in the appropriate symbolic terms.

The important link between Henry and the fox is a functional one. The animal symbol defines Henry's functional relation to the two feminine characters, and the pattern of identification established in the story serves to impersonalize that relation, to bring out its deep significance. The fox and the young man invade the mismanaged farm on different levels but in the same way. They are cunning, curious, and they are bound by all the forces of vital instinct to hunt out what they must possess in order to maintain themselves alive. The force that drives the fox to the henhouse is also the motivating force of Henry's savage quest. One action can, and in fact does, stand as a metaphor for the other. When Henry decides that he wants to marry March, we are told that "he would have to catch her as you catch a deer or a woodcock when you go out shooting." In this search it is less the true aim of the rifle that counts than a "supreme act of volition" which takes place in the soul of the hunter, a will which reaches out to master the will of the hunted even before the animal has come in sight. When Henry returns from camp to claim her, March looks at him with a "helpless, fascinated rabbit-look." And when Henry destroys Banford, he watches her twitching body with "intense bright eyes, as he would watch a wild goose he had shot."

The fox symbol more than anything else in the story clarifies the terms on which the action must be understood. Henry kills one woman and masters another because "it was what his life must have." Henry here is not "his life." The impulse to action is presented in this story as an influence which emanates from underneath or from beyond what we usually mean by the word "human." Henry, like the other characters, is a kind of form into which the life force wells. The form called Banford is somehow defective or diseased. No life wells up in her, and she must be discarded because her disease is catching. Life is the irreducible value, something to be served as well as enjoyed.

Does this story give a penetrating account of the relations of men and women under the conditions of a particular historical epoch? Most emphatically it does not. Furthermore, only a psychopathic reader could find anything in this story that he could use in his dealings with the opposite sex. "The Fox" is a mythical work of art which enacts life's unexplored morality. Henry demonstrates that morality and is its agent. Banford demonstrates the familiar condition of total alienation from man's instinctive source of being. In March we are free to find an image of ourselves. But her drastic rescue affords no clue to what we must do to save ourselves, any more than the story as a whole constitutes a blueprint for action.

The relation of a myth to its readers, at least in modern times, is always indirect. It invokes powers which are hardly manifest in the daily round of ordinary living. But even an unbeliever can be affected by a mythic work like "The Fox." It can provoke him to re-examine his assumptions about what is real, and it can force from him a grudging recognition that his little life is surrounded by a greater mystery. "The Fox" carries the reader to the limits of the known and suggests that something other than dead space lies beyond. It is an impressive artistic achievement in an area of experience where the expressive resources of an art form adapted by its conventions to a less intuitive exploration of reality are strained to the utmost.

"The Virgin and the Gypsy," published only posthumously but written around 1925 and set in a village of southern Derbyshire, grew out of a final visit Lawrence made to the Midlands in the middle nineteen-twenties. The Saywell family situation while recalling that of "Daughters of the Vicar" evokes much more directly the situation of the Weekly family after Frieda's elopement and divorce. Although the rector is not, and was never intended to be, an accurate portrait of Professor Weekly as a grass widower, the characters of Lucille and Yvette were surely based on Frieda's daughters, whom Lawrence had gotten to know and like when in adolescence they were permitted to visit their mother.

This retrospective quality is enhanced and reinforced by a number of elements in the story itself. The gypsy man Joe Boswell, "of a race that exists only to be harrying the outskirts of our society . . . and too wary to expose himself openly," who showed in his manner "the pride of the pariah, the half-sneering challenge of the outcast . . . and went his own way," belongs to the lurking, elusive tribe of Annable, Cicio, and Henry Grenfel, even though he also anticipates the "resurrected" groom, gamekeeper and

ex-soldier Oliver Mellors. The flash flood which destroys
the vicarage recalls the flood of *The Rainbow* which swept
Tom Brangwen out of life. Its cause—the collapse of a
reservoir dam undermined by an abandoned mine tunnel—
evokes the "bubbling up of under-darkness" of a tour-de-
force passage in *The Lost Girl* and reminds us, if we need
reminding, that Lawrence's holocausts are invariably affairs of destiny as well as "accidental." The destruction of
the house and its mistress Granny by rising and running water is life's inscrutable moral comment on the domestic
order over which Granny ruled.

But the most tantalizing backward turning comes in the
middle part of the story, in the brief episode involving
Major Charles Eastwood, where Eastwood explains how
he had known the gypsy during the war:

> Charles smoked for some moments.
> "That gypsy was the best man we had, with horses.
> Nearly died of pneumonia. I thought he *was* dead. He's a
> resurrected man to me. I'm a resurrected man myself, as
> far as that goes." He looked at Yvette. "I was buried for
> twenty hours under snow," he said. "And not much the
> worse for it, when they dug me out."
> There was a frozen pause in the conversation.
> "Life's awful!" said Yvette.
> "They dug me out by accident," he said.
> "Oh!———" Yvette trailed slowly. "It might be des-
> tiny, you know."
> To which he did not answer.   (*Short Novels*, II)

This northern, blond, blue-eyed winter sports enthusiast
is, of course, a resurrection of Gerald Crich. And the des-
tined accident of his death has been reimagined to allow
the possibility of a second life beyond the frozen wasteland
of the snow valley. Eastwood-Crich now believes that "desire is the most wonderful thing in life," and it goes with-

out saying that he is entirely dissociated from the morbid romance of big business. If a Gerald can be reborn to wholesome desire we begin to imagine other potential reconciliations. At a non-Euclidian point in infinity where opposed parallels meet we seem to see Clifford Chatterley rise from his motorized chair and stride off to join the little community of skippers and wood carvers that Connie and Mellors have established somewhere beyond civilization's alienating reaches. As in a glass darkly, we see the colliers of Bestwood-Eastwood dancing in a ring. In the Lawrence world grace usually does not, but always may, abound. Strictly speaking, *anyone* may come back to life.

Stories and plays built around the figure of the virgin girl, which enact her *rites du passage* into full womanhood, are frequent in literature and especially in English literature. The English virgin is an archetype through which that country's writers have expressed and re-expressed a communal ideal of the freshness and fullness of unimpeded life. Furthermore, the vicissitudes of the virgin in her successive avatars is always a revelation of the capacity of the society, at particular stages of development, to accommodate and embody this ideal. One measure of the health of Elizabethan society is the ease and grace with which the heroines of Shakespearian comedy surmount obstacles and reach their romantic and matrimonial goals: "Jack shall have Jill . . . and all shall be well."

Shakespeare wrote no plays like Middleton's *The Changeling*, whose theme is the spoliation and alienation of virgin innocence, evoking a society that is darkly aware of impending social and political disintegration. A century later, Richardson's *Pamela* celebrates the expanding middle class's sense of confident well-being, but Clarissa's agonies suggest how that well-being can be alienated by the hypertrophy of middle-class property and money instincts. The heroines of Jane Austen fulfill themselves through an exquisite and difficult adjustment between qualities of personality intrinsic to themselves and the complex patterns of a traditional landed society. When an Elizabeth marries a Darcy the heroine surrenders a measure of her unbounded spontaneity while the society surrenders a measure of its inflexibility. The metaphor of a formal dance suggests itself: wherein the beauty of the whole depends equally on the capacity of the dancer to move beautifully and on a traditional choreographic notation which determines the direction, tempo, rhythm, and limits of the movement.

This integration is lost as we move deeper into the industrial nineteenth century. Jane Eyre's triumphant settlement with Rochester is largely a matter of incredible luck. Like the ending of *Lucky Jim* it enacts a private fantasy of the unstatused; and one surmises that no flowers bloom on the grave of Helen Burns when Jane becomes legitimate mistress of Rochester's estate. The purity, faith, and warm-heartedness of Florence Dombey find no weak point at which the cold marble wall of her father's citadel of commercial enterprise can be breached. And so she retreats to the little room behind Sol Gills's shop where an anti-society of the aged, feeble-minded, clownish, and impotent forms around her. Eventually, her father arrives there too, but only after he has become impotent and poor. In effect, he has been flung over the wall yet the wall remains: the actual society continues indifferent to, and unfructified by Florence's *charisma*.

The fate, complexly rendered, of George Eliot's Gwendolen Harleth and of the virgin heroines of several of James's novels is spoliation in the context of a society of predators. Shaw's Major Barbara surrenders her generous illusions in exchange for a hard understanding of the capitalist system and its massive contradictions, but her disillusionment is mitigated by Shaw's underlying vision of the gradual change of a predatory society into a humanely planned socialist order which can accommodate Barbara's energy and idealism.

In a novel as recent as Kingsley Amis' *Take a Girl Like You* (1960) the virgin heroine reappears against the background of today's "affluent society." As Jenny Bunn blankly awaits the outcome of Patrick's frantic efforts to seduce her and submits numbly to near-rape at the end, one ponders the future of a society in which mere tropisms of behavior have replaced coherent relations of feelings to motives to actions. Mr. Amis' sad blank town, with its appalling roadhouse, rooming house, and public school, seems a part of the featureless contemporary wilderness where the characters of Samuel Beckett's plays and novels wander howling. The human value of the archetype vanishes in an environment populated, as *The Rainbow*'s Wiggiston was populated, by walking undead.

How do Lawrence's virgin stories fit into this tradition? Rather like Dickens in *Dombey and Son* he creates an antisociety with his gypsies, Italians, grooms, and gamekeepers. But these men are not impotent although they are often impoverished, sickly, and not overly intelligent. They lurk, but they also harry and undermine the social order from which they are alienated. However, their main effort is not directed at the destruction of society but rather toward rescuing the entrapped virgin, with her active complicity, from a society in process of destroying itself.

If the virgin is an ideal of the freshness and fullness of unimpeded life they serve the ideal by rescuing it from devastation, running off into darkness with the sacred flame, to light up another place whose whereabouts usually remains unknown. Cicio rescues Alvina from a milieu which has offered her physical desiccation and the gradual drying up of feeling as the only respectable career. Mellors restores Connie Chatterley's virginity by helping her to experience a resurrection of wholesome desire, and then rescues her from a milieu dominated by abstraction. Henry Grenfel breaks up the simulacrum of Nelly March's relationship with Banford and releases her virginal powers into the mainstream of life.

All these victories over an unwholesome society are similar, and we may wonder what "The Virgin and the Gypsy" does that is different and distinct. In the first place, the fresh, insouciant, adolescent Yvette stands in the same relation to these older, wearier, and even somewhat shopworn heroines as true virgin to *demi-vierge*. Also, she is more intelligent and of a finer temperament; therefore, Lawrence's account of her character is intrinsically more interesting, while her maneuverings to maintain her integrity are inevitably more complex, less unwitting, and less desperate. The climax of Yvette's adventure with Joe Boswell is neither a ceremonious defloration nor elopement into the permanent exile of an unknown land. Although stricken with longing for "her gypsy of the world's-end night" Yvette reposes at the end in the bosom of her family. With Granny gone she and Lucille may well be able to break up and reform the patterns of Saywell family life from a position inside, thus avoiding the tragedy of permanent alienation from their society and the obvious discomforts of housekeeping in a horse-drawn caravan.

A further distinction of "The Virgin and the Gypsy" is that here Lawrence gives his most coherent picture of the actual processes of "mutual interdestructivity" as they work themselves out within a social unit that is representatively middle class, respectable, and cultured. Disintegration is not a mere *donné*, for it is constantly enacted in encounters between Granny and her daughter, the vicar and his mother, between any of the older members of the family and the two young girls. The stale air of the rectory is charged with a murderous potential of static electricity, heavy with poison fumes of hatred. Lawrence brings this diseased condition of life home to us concretely, analyzes it fully, and for once explains the aetiology of the disease.

The characteristic vice of the older Saywells, their constitutional defect, is emotional phoniness. Each is a born liar about what he or she is actually feeling at a given time, and each lies not only to others but to himself. The rector has been deeply shocked and hurt by his wife's elopement but has failed to work through these feelings. Instead he has constructed two images of the woman who deserted him, one of the pure young wife who had once shared his bed and board, another of an utterly depraved creature who ran off in order to indulge monstrous sexual appetites. These images cannot be coherently related to each other or to the actual Cynthia, but they operate effectively as a barrier against self-recognition. Perhaps the rector would like to kill Cynthia; maybe he would like her to come back; perhaps deep down he knows that he was partially or wholly to blame for the failure of his marriage. Who knows? Certainly not the rector. His "skulking self-love" precludes the possibility of a submission to the suffering necessarily entailed in coming to grips with one's own deepest feelings. It is this same self-love which Granny exploits in her take-over of the family.

Granny is Lawrence's most loathsome image of a woman dominated by the will to power. She is also the most deliberate, crafty and skillful liar in a family of liars, holding and extending her power by constant intrusive manipulation. She manipulates her traditional social role of the English mater or mum, to whom a tribute of loyalty is customarily due, to make the family "her own extended ego."

She manipulates her son into a stagnant subservience by playing upon his self-love, manipulates Aunt Cissie, her daughter, until she has reduced her to a slave whose time is wholly taken up with catering to Granny's slothful and gluttonous appetites. Everything is grist for her mill of exploitation, even her own hardness of hearing. Where she encounters resistance to her will, as she is bound to with Yvette and Lucille, she hates; and when she is caught out, as she is in the mirror-breaking scene, she does not hesitate to lie her way into the clear, coolly and consciously.

Granny, as the narrator points out, is a toad, an obscene idol, a sheer horror, and yet she is as real and contemporary as stale Yorkshire pudding or American advertisements for family fall-out shelters. She is a nightmare of the respectable middle classes, her bulk and power feeding upon the moral cowardice of typical members of that class, a cowardice manifesting itself chiefly in the realm of fundamental emotional dishonesty.

If Granny is the most skilled liar, Aunt Cissie is the least skilled. An old maid approaching fifty, she uses the ideal of humble, selfless Christian service as a barrier against intense feelings of physical and emotional frustration, but the feelings break through in frequent episodes of inchoate rage. Inevitably her favorite target for rage is Yvette, whose detachment, carelessness of consequences, and sexual aura arouse her deepest jealousy. Aunt Cissie aspires to a sanctity and blamelessness of life for which she has no natural talent; both she herself and the people around her must take the consequences.

These three, in implicit alliance with mute, dingy Uncle Fred, arraign themselves against the younger girls, seeking by a perverse instinct to draw them into the family orbit of emotional dishonesty. Lucille's resistance, while genuine, is badly calculated to protect her integrity. By fixing her life in the rigid routines of a commuting London office worker and by stoically disciplining herself to become inattentive to the household atmosphere, she hopes to ride out the storm. The danger of this tactic is that it represents a denial of feeling comparable to her own father's denial, and may in time bring about the sort of self-betrayal for which all her older relatives have such abundance of talent. Thus, about half-way through the story she confesses to Yvette that connection with men through sex strikes her as hateful and horrible:

> "How horrible it sounds: *connect us with men!*" cried Lucille, with revulsion. "Wouldn't you hate to be connected with men, that way? Oh I think it's an awful pity there has to *be* sex! It would be so much better if we could still be men and women, without that sort of thing."
>
> (*Short Novels*, II)

The key word here is "connect." When the connection between deep feeling and consciousness is broken or weakened within the self, there is a revulsion against the idea of direct connection to another that the sex relation assumes, *and in time* a growing incapacity to connect with reality itself. This further point is brought out in the terrible scene where the rector orders Yvette to stop seeing the Eastwoods. He begins with the intention of warning her away from some unconventional people but his imagination is soon overwhelmed by a mad fantasy in which the Eastwoods and his daughter are implicated in "horrors": ' "Say no more!" he said in a low, hissing voice. "But I will kill you before you go the way of your mother." ' Here the rector's readiness to transform actuality into lubricious melodrama is at once comic and disgusting. Yvette, bewildered and benumbed by her father's violence, still cannot respond to him in these terms. She says, "Do you mean I mustn't know the Eastwoods?" which is no doubt what he does mean in his self-corrupted and language-corrupting fashion. Yvette is a natural connector, her carelessness, frivolity, and apparently selfish indifference to the pseudo-feelings of her elders nicely calculated to preserve the free flow and interchange within herself of natural impulse, feeling, and conscious thought. But without some experience of connection outside this diseased household it will only be a matter of time before she succumbs to corruption and learns to reply to her father's snakelike hissing with a melodramatic hiss of her own. Although the Eastwoods, to whom she responds immediately and without self-consciousness, afford her access to a world that is not hag-ridden by grey respectability, it is the direct, naked, elemental connection with the gypsy which saves her life, strengthening her beyond the possibility of a renewed imprisonment.

In their relation Yvette and Boswell ignore differences of social status, the existence of Boswell's gypsy wife (with her apparent consent), and dispense with all those elaborated exchanges of fine phrases which the rector, who is, we are told, a distinguished writer and lecturer, would deem suitable to courtship. They are alone with each other on only two occasions, once at the caravan and once in bed together in the flooded rectory, and neither time is sexual consummation possible. Yet they save each other's lives by intertwining against the freezing cold which rises from the river waters, and it is the gypsy's touch upon her that opens for Yvette "undiscovered doors to life." At the end it seems that the fate of the virgin is to be neither spoliation nor exile. For once Lawrence, in a conciliatory mood that visited him very seldom after he had written *Women in Love*, lets stand a direct connection between the deepest forces of life and an actual social order. Through an opened door surges inward upon society a great cleansing flood of wholesome feeling in which the abstracted and desiccated are washed away, while the saving remnant disport and renew themselves as though they bathed in the waters of Jordan.

CONCLUSION

CONCLUSION

IN DISCUSSIONS of the modern novel Lawrence's work is sometimes categorized as "poetic." The term is woefully imprecise when applied to novels and may suggest a sentimental effusiveness to which Lawrence's fiction is totally alien; yet there seems to be one sense in which it is appropriate. That is, when I try to bring to mind his fiction as a whole, and to experience directly his special quality, I find I am thinking more of certain powerful, pervading images than of modes of characterization and style, narrative strategies, or reiterated moral doctrines and themes. The images supply poetic analogues for the essence of Lawrence's creative drive to master and transform human reality, analogues too for those elements of his imagination that were corrosive, iconoclastic, even nihilistic. Moreover they both organize and are organized by the novels and stories which give them fictive substance.

The image of crossing a gulf to the shore of an unknown land adumbrates Lawrence's vision of the search for a transformation of being and a deep change of heart. Man's effort to enter fully into the state of self-possession from which he finds himself estranged in the modern world is imaged as a perilous journey. One recalls Paul Morel moving across the gulf of night toward the lights of the town or the ravaged Man who had died launching his little boat at dusk into the Mediterranean Sea. Our estrangement from ourselves and our loss of touch with one another under the conditions of a mechanistic civilization are represented through the image of the lobster shell of insentience or, again, through the image of a binding integument which constrains and suffocates life. The effort to break out of this constraint may be represented as the breaking of an integument:

The air all seemed rare and different. Suddenly the world had become quite different: as if some skin or integument had broken, as if the old, mouldering London sky had crackled and rolled back, like an old skin, shrivelled, leaving an absolutely new blue heaven.

("The Last Laugh," *Complete Short Stories*, III, 641)

And the agony of a man whose psychic defenses against intimacy have been breached may be represented as the breaking of a calcareous shell:

He had one desire—to escape from this intimacy, this friendship, which had been thrust upon him. He could not bear it that he had been touched by the blind man, his insane reserve broken in. He was like a mollusc whose shell is broken.

("The Blind Man," *Complete Short Stories*, II, 365)

Yet more often the breaking of shell or integument is conjoined with the image of a deep inner livingness—"some passionate vision . . . embedded in the half dead body of this life . . . the quick body within the dead" ("Glad Ghosts")—that has survived the deliberate cultivation of insentience, the ravages of the abstracted will and its ingenious machinery, and can be released to enliven the existence of an individual or a society. This seemingly miraculous and unlooked for release comes most often when someone puts himself into poignant sensory contact with something or someone concretely, essentially alive: when a Lady Chatterley, as she watches the gamekeeper wash himself in the open air, feels in her womb "the warm, white flame of a single life, revealing itself in contours that one might touch"; when Paul Morel finds the lilies flagging all loose in his mother's garden on a moonlit night; when Elizabeth Bates, tragically and paradoxically, recovers a true vision of her husband's living identity while tracing the contours of his dead body with her hands and lips.

These images aim at the preservation of a free, unbounded vitality in the face of multifold threats to life
offered by an iron age of destructive machines and abstracted systems. But there is one other image in Lawrence's work which adumbrates the condition of deathliness
itself with magnificent and compelling power. It is the
image of the void or gulf into which anyone may fall while
seeking to control his destiny and salvage his integrity amid
the arrayed threats and promises of contemporary experience. It is represented by the endless night which confronts
Paul at the end of *Sons and Lovers*; most powerfully in
the snow void, mirroring the disintegration of Gerald Crich
and the whole society from which he comes, at the end of
Women in Love; most horribly in the calculated blankness
of Cathcart's third island universe.

Finally, there is an image set apart from the others by
reason of its strangeness and incoherence. In "The Ladybird" it is referred to as "the indecipherable image of mastery" and designates that relationship of power, sometimes
between man and woman but more often between man and
man, to which Lawrence gave close attention in the leadership novels and to which he adverted from time to time in
other books as well. The image is actualized variously: for
example, in the weird keening night song of Count Dionys
Psanek; in the ceremonious assassination of the woman who
rode away; in the wrestling match between Birkin and
Crich. More often than not it appears in association with
rancorously anti-democratic political arguments, with invalidism or actual sickness, with situations of male friendship that are heavily tinged with homoerotic feeling, with
episodes involving gross physical violence or actual murder.

This bizarre concatenation does not yield to rational
analysis any more readily than the famous Shakespearian
image cluster of kites with carrion with melting sweets with

THE DEED OF LIFE

spaniels with the sore heels of courtiers. It was Lawrence's habit to put everything of himself into his books. This was his greatest strength and also guaranteed that anything unresolved or regressive in his feeling and thinking would turn up in the work. That he became disenchanted with the leadership ideal after writing *The Plumed Serpent* is well known. Yet the indecipherable images of *Apocalypse* (1930) show that the theme returned, like a ghostly King Charles's Head, to haunt him as he fought his losing battle with advanced tuberculosis. Perhaps Lawrence's experiences of severe physical illness provide the key after all. The image may embody a compensatory fantasy bred out of the agonizing frustrations of protracted and recurring sickness that fleshed itself in a man of extraordinary vitality. Too little is known of the psychic effects of chronic disease to pursue the question further.

One's final objection to the image of mastery is that it is never converted into an instrument of vision. Lawrence's work and life, like Dostoevsky's, seem to show two utterly contrasted impulses: an impulse to build life anew and a counterimpulse to stand aside and let the world go smash. Lawrence complained perpetually of the frustration of his "societal" impulse and badgered his friends with successive schemes for the establishment of a utopian colony; yet most of his adult life was conducted as a series of strategic withdrawals from society, while his few attempts to realize his utopia proved disastrous. Speaking for life, and for a kind of sacred self-fulfilling participation in the human community, he lived closer to death and more intensely isolated than any other major modern writer, and he came to understand the void—the career of disintegration—by attending to some of the deepest impulses in his own soul. At the very height of his first happiness with Frieda, he wrote to

Edward Garnett from Lago Di Garda,[1] "It always fright-ens me how life gets reduced down to fewer elements the further one goes: Captain Scott had cold, hunger, and death. I've got love."

A decade and a half later this painful self-appraisal is transformed into the lucid and objective exploration of the impulse to reduce life that Cathcart's career illustrates. "The Man Who Loved Islands" shows us what we must do and what we must not do if we, and by implication our society, are not to smother in abstraction. Lawrence, by coming to terms with a profoundly negative feeling inside himself, acquired the knowledge and earned the right to point out the elements of deathliness in the social and per-sonal relationships of the rest of us. He did not, however, come similarly to terms with his power obsession, which remains mere incoherent, unauthoritative fantasy from first to last.

If Lawrence is to be aligned with one particular tradition in the novel it must be the tradition of those nineteenth-century artists like Tolstoi, Melville, Dostoevsky—and Proust somewhat later—who experience the profound spir-itual contradictions and tensions of their age as a perpetual torment of their own spiritual and physical substance, who offer themselves to us simultaneously as leaders and as scapegoats. Like Moses, they direct us toward the promised land of a transformation of being and usually die exhausted at the very moment it is rumored that the desert has been crossed.

Among twentieth-century novelists Lawrence is set apart by virtue of the orientation of his entire body of work toward the future, rather than toward the dead past or the contingencies of the immediate present; and by his aware-

[1] 18 February 1913. See *The Collected Letters of D. H. Lawrence*, ed. Harry T. Moore (New York: Viking, 1962), I, 186.

ness that modern men can recover from the material and spiritual devastations of industrial civilization only by creating a human community that is suffused with reverence for life. His notion of fate, touched upon at many points in this book, and which operates in his fiction as a central principle of form, holds that men contain within themselves their own vital freedom. As men move through life and enter into relations with the world they are from instant to instant spelling out the terms of their fulfillment or their eventual undoing. In this process even accidental happenings become revelations of a destiny which continuously composes itself. The doctrine is anything but pessimistic, since it dispenses altogether with the idea of a predetermined pattern and assumes that with even a single instant left a man may snatch his soul from the void and find life.

Lawrence intends that the same idea should be applied to the career of a whole society or civilization, and it happens that we stand at a juncture of history where his idea may soon be given tragic verification. If, a few months or years from now, our world is destroyed by nuclear war, it will be the revelation of a destiny that has composed itself from moment to moment over all the generations since the onset of the Industrial Revolution. Such a searing epiphany of the underlying deathliness of a great civilization would be final and definitive, even were it to be shown that the first aggressive missile was launched by mistake—perhaps owing to a mechanical failure for which no one was responsible. Nevertheless, the free choice of life still remains, and will remain until the last instant before the first war rocket describes its pure, inhuman arc across space.

INDEX

227

OTHER TITLES IN LITERATURE
AVAILABLE IN PRINCETON AND
PRINCETON/BOLLINGEN PAPERBACKS

THE IDEA OF A THEATER, by Francis Fergusson (#126), $1.95

THE JAPANESE TRADITION IN BRITISH AND AMERICAN LITERATURE, by Earl Miner (#59), $2.95

JOSEPH CONRAD: A Psychoanalytic Biography, by Bernard C. Meyer, M.D. (#188), $2.95

THE LIMITS OF ART: Vol. 1, From Homer to Chaucer, edited by Huntington Cairns (P/B #179), $3.95

THE LIMITS OF ART: Vol. 2, From Villon to Gibbon, edited by Huntington Cairns (P/B #203), $3.95

THE LIMITS OF ART: Vol. 3, From Goethe to Joyce, edited by Huntington Cairns (P/B #217), $3.95

LINGUISTICS AND LITERARY HISTORY: Essays in Stylistics, by Leo Spitzer (#88), $2.95

THE LYRICAL NOVEL: Studies in Hermann Hesse, André Gide, and Virginia Woolf (#62), $2.95

MIMESIS: The Representation of Reality in Western Literature, by Erich Auerbach, translated by Willard R. Trask (#124), $2.95

NEWTON DEMANDS THE MUSE, by Marjorie Hope Nicolson (#31), $2.95

NOTES ON PROSODY and ABRAM GANNIBAL, by Vladimir Nabokov (P/B #184), $2.95

THE NOVELS OF FLAUBERT, by Victor Brombert (#164), $2.95

THE NOVELS OF HERMANN HESSE, by Theodore Ziolkowski (#68), $2.95

ON WORDSWORTH'S "PRELUDE," by Herbert Lindenberger (#55), $2.95

ON THE ILIAD, by Rachel Bespaloff, translated by Mary McCarthy (P/B #218), $1.45

THE POETIC ART OF W. H. AUDEN, by John G. Blair (#65), $1.95

THE POETICAL WORKS OF EDWARD TAYLOR, edited by Thomas H. Johnson (#32), $2.95

THE POWER OF SATIRE: Magic, Ritual, Art, by Robert C. Elliott (#61), $2.95

A PREFACE TO CHAUCER, by D. W. Robertson, Jr. (#178), $4.95

PREFACES TO SHAKESPEARE, by Harley Granville-Barker (#23, 24, 25, 26), $2.95 each

THE PROSE OF OSIP MANDELSTAM, translated by Clarence Brown (#67), $2.95

RADICAL INNOCENCE: The Contemporary American Novel, by Ihab Hassan (#237), $2.95

RELIGIOUS HUMANISM AND THE VICTORIAN NOVEL: George Eliot, Walter Pater, and Samuel Butler, by U. C. Knoepflmacher (#187), $2.95